"*Can't Buy Me Love?* Over 100 million albums sold say otherwise. Sam Staley uses the lens of economics as your *Ticket to Ride* from *Penny Lane* to *Taxman*. You can't buy love ... but you can buy this book!"

— *Professor Dirk Mateer, University of Arizona, USA*

"Sam Staley's new book does something unique: It explains core principles of cultural entrepreneurship, not by statistical analysis (as in the research literature) or by sketchy anecdotes, but by a sustained, detailed analysis of a team of cultural entrepreneurs, namely the Beatles. As such, it fills an important gap in modern writing on cultural economics and entrepreneurship. The book is extremely well-written, and although it makes use of much economics and management theory it is highly accessible."

— *Professor Nicolai Foss, Copenhagen Business School, Denmark*

"Sam Staley's book is thought provoking and well written. It will be a good addition to the Beatles book shelf."

— *Todd Lowry, Former Director of Business and Legal Affairs,*
Hal Leonard Company, musician, and arranger of
The Complete Beatles

"If you think business is just money and greed, you'll be sadly oblivious to most of what goes on in the world. In *The Beatles and Economics*, Sam Staley explains that even in the business end of arts and culture, exciting and even inspirational developments define daily life. For both personal fulfillment and a flourishing, vibrant society, nothing beats economic freedom."

— *Lawrence W. Reed, President Emeritus, Foundation for Economic Education, USA*

THE BEATLES AND ECONOMICS

The Beatles are considered the most influential popular music act of the twentieth century, widely recognized for their influence on popular culture. The inability of other bands and artists to imitate their fame has prompted questions such as: How did the Beatles become so successful? What factors contributed to their success? Why did they break up?

The Beatles and Economics: Entrepreneurship, Innovation, and the Making of a Cultural Revolution answers these questions using the lens of economic analysis. Economics provides the prism for explaining why their success—while legendary in scale—is not mythic. This book explores how the band's commercial achievements were intimately tied to the larger context of economic globalization and rebuilding post-World War II. It examines how the Beatles' time in Hamburg is best understood as an investment in human capital, and why the entrepreneurial growth mindset was critical to establishing a scalable market niche and sustaining the Beatles' ability to lead and shape emerging markets in entertainment and popular music. Later chapters consider how the economics of decision-making and organizational theory helps us to understand the band's break-up at its economic peak.

This essential text is of interest to anyone interested in the economic dynamics and social forces that shape cultural change.

Samuel R. Staley, PhD, is director of the DeVoe L. Moore Center in the College of Social Sciences and Public Policy at Florida State University, USA, where he teaches economics and social entrepreneurship.

ROUTLEDGE ECONOMICS AND POPULAR CULTURE SERIES

Series Editor: **J. Brian O'Roark**, Robert Morris University, USA

Broadway and Economics
Economic Lessons from Show Tunes
Matthew C. Rousu

Dystopia and Economics
A Guide to Surviving Everything from the Apocalypse to Zombies
Edited by Charity-Joy Revere Acchiardo and Michelle Albert Vachris

Contemporary Film and Economics
Lights! Camera! Econ!
Samuel R. Staley

Superheroes and Economics
The Shadowy World of Capes, Masks and Invisible Hands
Edited by J. Brian O'Roark and Rob Salkowitz

The Beatles and Economics
Entrepreneurship, Innovation, and the Making of a Cultural Revolution
Samuel R. Staley

War Movies and Economics
Lessons from Hollywood's Adaptations of Military Conflict
Edited by Laura J. Ahlstrom and Franklin G. Mixon, Jr.

For more information about this series, please visit www.routledge.com/Routledge-Economics-and-Popular-Culture-Series/book-series/REPC

THE BEATLES AND ECONOMICS

Entrepreneurship, Innovation, and the Making of a Cultural Revolution

Samuel R. Staley

Routledge
Taylor & Francis Group

LONDON AND NEW YORK

First published 2020
by Routledge
2 Park Square, Milton Park, Abingdon, Oxon OX14 4RN

and by Routledge
52 Vanderbilt Avenue, New York, NY 10017

Routledge is an imprint of the Taylor & Francis Group, an informa business

British Library Cataloguing-in-Publication Data
A catalogue record for this book is available from the British Library

Library of Congress Cataloging-in-Publication Data
Names: Staley, Sam, 1961- author.
Title: The Beatles and economics : entrepreneurship, innovation, and the making of a cultural revolution / Samuel R. Staley.
Description: [1.] | New York : Routledge, 2020. |
Series: Routledge economics and popular culture |
Includes bibliographical references and index.
Identifiers: LCCN 2019056993 (print) | LCCN 2019056994 (ebook) |
ISBN 9781138363526 (hardback) | ISBN 9781138363540 (paperback) |
ISBN 9780429431586 (ebook)
Subjects: LCSH: Beatles. | Popular music--Economic aspects. | Economics.
Classification: LCC ML421.B4 S677 2020 (print) |
LCC ML421.B4 (ebook) | DDC 782.42166092/2--dc23
LC record available at https://lccn.loc.gov/2019056993
LC ebook record available at https://lccn.loc.gov/2019056994

ISBN: 978-1-138-36352-6 (hbk)
ISBN: 978-1-138-36354-0 (pbk)
ISBN: 978-0-429-43158-6 (ebk)

Typeset in Bembo
by Taylor & Francis Books

To Chip Staley

CONTENTS

FIGURES

ABOUT THE AUTHOR

Samuel R. Staley, PhD, in addition to playing Beatles songs on his guitar, is on the full-time faculty of the College of Social Sciences and Public Policy at Florida State University (FSU) and is director of the DeVoe L. Moore Center, an applied public policy research center focused on state and local public policy issues. In addition to his academic appointments, he has helped to co-found two public policy think tanks, held leadership positions in numerous nonprofit organizations ranging from research director to president/CEO, and chaired the board of directors for several civic groups. While at FSU, he helped to build the social entrepreneurship curriculum in the College of Social Sciences and Public Policy and co-chaired the SE curriculum development committee for the Jim Moran School of Entrepreneurship. He has taught introductory, upper division, and master's-level courses in economics at FSU, the University of Dayton, and Wright State University.

Sam's popular writing has appeared in numerous outlets intended for general audiences, including the *New York Times*, the *Washington Post*, the *Los Angeles Times, Reason* magazine, *Planning* magazine, and the *National Review*. His research has been published by leading academic journals, including *Transportation Research Part A, Housing Policy Debate, Town Planning Review, Journal of the American Planning Association, Economics of Education Review*, and *Journal of Transportation Engineering*.

The author of 13 books, Dr. Staley's fiction and non-fiction books have earned top awards in a wide range of categories, including published education and information, current affairs/politics, historical fiction, young adult fiction, and published mainstream/literary fiction. His most recent books include *Contemporary Film and Economics* (Routledge, 2018) and *Calusa Spirits* (SYP Publishing, 2018), the third book in the Pirate of Panther Bay trilogy.

He earned his PhD from The Ohio State University, MS from Wright State University, and BA from Colby College. He was a Bradley Fellow in the Center for Study of Public Choice at George Mason University while pursuing doctoral studies in economics from 1989 to 1990.

PREFACE

Perhaps the most common question heard while writing this book was the following: Does the world really need another book about the Beatles? The question is a fair one, given the volumes that have been written and interviews recorded over the past decades. The answer would have been "no" if not for a drive from Tallahassee, Florida to Nashville, Tennessee during the summer of 2017. Sirius XM had just launched the Beatles Channel, and its DJs were promoting the 50th anniversary of the path-breaking album *Sgt. Pepper's Lonely Hearts Club Band*. In the middle of the interviews, a basic question kept coming to the forefront of my thoughts: How did the Beatles accomplish this feat?

As an economist, all the usual explanations—talent, popularity, serendipity, commercial opportunism—fell flat. The album project was too big, too inventive, too adventurous, too *expensive* to be explained by conventional cultural, social, or even psychological theories. The album was so far ahead of its time, recording labels would not be able to accurately score its financial risk. Its experimental nature meant no one could forecast whether it would doom the Beatles, represent a short-term diversion of their careers, or unleash a new wave of musical experimentation, innovation, and artistry. The answer today is clear, but in 1966 when they started recording the first songs for the album, no one had a clear understanding of the potential impact. No one could have.

That night, my brother, a musician and business owner in Nashville, loaned me legendary recording engineer Geoff Emerick's memoir *Here, There and Everywhere*. Going inside the black box of the Beatles, no one apparently had tried to unpack the economics behind the Beatles' creative process, or how economic forces might have shaped the choices they made. No one really seemed to have a good grip on why John Lennon, Paul McCartney, George Harrison, and Ringo Starr were allowed to turn very expensive property on Abbey Road in London into a giant laboratory for a project that what would become an unprecedented, disrupting impact on pop music. It was an extravagant indulgence allowed by executives at EMI records by what many would have considered at the time as a quintessentially capitalist enterprise. From this starting point, a commentary published by the Independent Institute in Oakland, California was followed by a presentation at an academic conference, and a pitch to Routledge as part of their Economics and Popular Culture series. Yes, indeed, it seemed, another book would have value. *The Beatles and Economics* was born.

Importantly, *The Beatles and Economics* does not offer new historical tidbits or gossip about how the Beatles worked as individuals or interacted with each other. This book does not dive into artistic critiques, dissect song lyrics, take swipes as artists or their fans, or even speculate about the role art plays in popular culture. The value in economics is how we look at and interpret the data, not in how we collect it. The story that unfolds in the following pages is built by relying on well-researched and what are in many cases standard accounts of the band, the individuals, and the social and cultural forces at work. What *The Beatles and Economics* provides is a fresh way to look at this information, weaving together dots in a pattern that appeared to have been unexplored until now. As the following chapters suggest, this fresh perspective leads to some startling conclusions and questions about much of the conventional wisdom surrounding the origins of the band, the internal group dynamics, and the implications for pop music, culture, and industry.

Economics most fundamentally is a lens, a framework, through which human choices are made. Sometimes these decisions are small, or micro, as in the case of when individuals such as John Lennon, Paul McCartney, George Harrison, or Ringo Starr decided to stay in (or leave) the band. Sometimes these choices are shaped by larger events, such as the groundswell of wealth creation lifting a new generation from the ravages of economic depression and world war. This economic lens turns out to provide very new ways of looking at the Beatles phenomenon.

This book also purposely takes a relatively narrow focus. Many books on the Beatles tend to be exhaustive biographies or histories. This book pulls the salient facts together to weave a complex story in a focused way. The default is to reference general and well-known facts or events in order to keep the prose and the narrative as straightforward and clean as possible. The book is not intending to add to the canon of Beatles history. Rather, *The Beatles and Economics* is motivated by a key consideration: What factors led to the rise of The Beatles and their sustained influence fifty years after they broke up?

This story is as fascinating as it is dynamic. This book is as much about innovation as it is about one of pop culture's most iconic symbols. The economic lens helps answer this question as well as coax insight from their story to understand why some enterprises are able to sustain their creative drive while others falter. The analysis helps deconstruct the impact of the Beatles' experience in practical terms and explain why their impact may be legendary, by not necessarily mythic. At the end of the day, the Beatles were ordinary men with extraordinary drive and ambition. They were not naturally gifted musicians or obvious pop music idols. They lacked formal education and existed at the margins or near margins of society during a very difficult period of modern English history. Their success provides lessons for all entrepreneurs.

Finally, a note on sources. In keeping with an attempt to ensure the text is as jargon-free and as accessible as possible to the non-economist, sourcing has been limited to what is absolutely necessary. When possible, sources and references are built directly into the narrative. At the end of each chapter is a list of primary references. Data and information that were verified by at least three independent sources are typically unsourced in this book. In these cases, however, most of the information can be found in one or more of the works cited at the end of each chapter. In a few instances, Wikipedia is used as a primary source. These instances are noted. Even in these cases, however, most of the data have been independently validated. Readers are encouraged to contact the author directly if they have specific questions about source material or conclusions reached through the economic analysis via email at sstaley@fsu.edu.

1

THE BLACK SWAN OF POPULAR MUSIC?

Economic concepts: Human capital, entrepreneurship, growth mindset, economic growth, resource optimization, innovation

The Beatles, as a band, existed for not much more than a decade, but their influence remains unprecedented in popular music. They scored more top ten hits than any other band during their run, and their music inspired countless artists. Overestimating their influence is almost impossible. Yet John Lennon, the band's founder and driving force, was dismissive of their contribution to popular music, famously stating in an interview, "The Beatles were just a band that made it very, very big. That's all."

In historical perspective, Lennon's statement is almost laughable. As a group, the Beatles have sold more than 800 million albums. It also has the most number one hits on Billboard's Hot 100 (with 20). As individual musicians, Lennon, Paul McCartney, George Harrison, and Ringo Starr represent four of the fourteen individuals inducted into the Rock and Roll Hall of Fame as solo acts as well as members of a band.

Lennon, however, was correct in one sense: the Beatles' success, while legendary in scale and influence, was not of mythic proportions. The Beatles and its individual members had many attributes in common with many other bands at their time. However, they also fell short on many measures of artistic accomplishment and, initially, even competence. Lennon was also correct in recognizing that the band's early commercial success was driven in large part by an economic wave unknown in human history and benefited from more than a little serendipity.

But the band's iconic status in popular culture and music was not sealed by these events or elements. The Beatles, as individuals and as a group, also had to make critical decisions at various points to maintain the momentum of their careers. They also had to invest in continuous innovation in order to stay at the forefront of artistic and commercial success. These decisions were intentional, not random, and involved a great deal of conscious choice, evaluations of alternative uses of resources, and even cost-benefit analysis. They faced many decisions that involved significant trade-offs about how they would use their time, their money, and their reputations. These decisions were fundamentally economic in nature—deciding on the best course of action based on limited resources in an uncertain environment. They also implicitly and explicitly made these decisions in a market system, allowing supply, demand, and market prices to guide their decisions and trajectory. This book explores these kinds of decisions and their implications.

This book also draws on new concepts from economics, entrepreneurship studies, and strategic management to provide insight into why the Beatles were able to foster continuous innovation, translate the innovation into commercial success, and how the internal dynamic of the band encouraged this innovation as well as sowed the seeds for its demise. The band was organized for a particular purpose—to combine resources and talents to produce popular music. It was an important vehicle for leveraging their talents as well as developing services that consumers of their products would be willing to buy. They used the band to monetize their artistic talents.

Were the Beatles a black swan?

While the Beatles as a band has taken on mythic status, *The Beatles and Economics* examines its organizational structure to explore its benefits as well as its limits. Undoubtedly, the band provided critical advantages to its members and allowed them to both excel creatively as well as commercially. This role is very similar to a business in other industries. But as the members—the human capital assets that make up the band—matured and evolved, the organizational structure constrained them in important ways. The friction and arguments that plagued the band in its waning years may be best understood when viewed through this lens than the more conventional approach which focuses on interpersonal feuds, social pressures, and purely artistic differences. Thus, *The Beatles and Economics* may well break new ground in understanding the internal dynamics of innovative enterprises and the management of creatives within entrepreneurial organizational frameworks.

The Beatles, of course, were far more than "just a band." As individuals, they fused a tremendous investment in natural talent and skill—what economists call human capital—with a "growth mindset." This allowed them to push the frontiers of popular music and leverage the rising incomes of the post-World War II period into a global financial juggernaut that continues to be felt well into the twenty-first century. This entrepreneurial drive and energy were in evidence as early as their formative years attending secondary school in Liverpool. In fact, even the band's culture was set early, before they began their now famous "residencies" in Hamburg, Germany which many believe was the critical jumping off point for their future success. The band that became the bestselling act in the UK and the US, charting more top ten hits than any other act over a ten-year period, established its culture and dynamic when John Lennon formed one of the more than 300 "skiffle" groups called The Quarrymen in the mid-1950s.

The outsized influence of the Beatles on popular music might well tempt some to label their impact as a black swan event. Nassim Taleb defined a black swan as an event so unexpected that it can't be forecast but has a game-changing impact on everything. The impact fundamentally reshapes the industry and the economy. By many measures, the Beatles phenomenon had these impacts. Popular music was fundamentally transformed between the time the Beatles conducted their first tour to the US in 1964 and the year they formally broke up in 1970. Wikipedia, an indicator of popular tastes and trends, lists just seven major musical genres in the US under the entry "1950s in music"—Rock and roll, classic pop, R&B, blues, country, jazz, and folk. By the 1980s, popular music had splintered into a dizzying array of variation as rock music spawned subgenres such as heavy metal, alternative rock, arena rock and new major genres such as electronic music and hip hop became mainstream. The Beatles were at the forefront of this explosion in tastes and variation, writing, releasing, and producing songs that contributed to 60 major music genres and subgenres. They were not just an early adopter. They were innovators, laying critical foundations for an explosion in creativity and experimentation in popular music felt 50 years after their band's official break up.

But were the Beatles a black swan? This book uses the lens of economics to argue they were not. While the band benefited from events beyond their control, the personalities and its internal culture created a formal, recognizable framework for identifying new opportunities, exploiting them, and optimizing their value in a dynamic context. Their innovation was a by-product of entrepreneurial ambition, intrapreneurial organizational culture, and larger social (and economic) forces that allowed them to continue to push their industry forward. The result was unheard of commercial success and a fundamental restructuring of the industry.

The Beatles and World War II

The immediate aftermath of World War II is critical to understanding the revolutionary shifts in popular music in the 1960s and 1970s. Six years of total war had devastated much of the European continent, including England, France, and Germany. Cataclysmic is too soft a word. Everyone was employed in the war effort. Accurate and meaningful economic statistics do not exist because their collection was not a priority. Wage income for consumer goods provided little value since resources were directed toward waging total war. Markets, as most people know them, simply didn't exist.

The terror of war was a daily part of life. Liverpool was bombed 80 times by the German air force and was ground zero for the Battle of the Atlantic as Germany tried to strangle Great Britain through relentless submarine and air attacks on merchant shipping. Thousands of Liverpudlians died in these bombings, which eventually made the city the second most bombed city in the country, after London. Julia Lennon dodged German bombs running through the streets of Liverpool during an air raid in order to deliver John in a hospital in 1940. Significantly, John Lennon's middle name is taken from the indefatigable wartime prime minister, Winston Churchill. John, Paul, George, and Ringo grew up around the bombed-out shells of buildings and churches as part of their everyday life.

Yet, this context is rarely discussed in the biographies of the Beatles. In part, this is likely because the war was over by the time the Beatles were old enough to be aware of the hardships and terrors their parents endured. As boys in their pre-teen and teenage years, they were focused on what most children prioritize—discovering their talents, finding friends, and learning about the opposite sex. Indeed, nothing in the biographies of these four "lads" from Liverpool suggest they were interested in much more. With the possible exception of McCartney, they were not groomed for England's elite universities, or expected to become titans of industry. Their hearts were set on a decidedly less stable profession from an early age—pop musicians. They craved the stage, the limelight, and the girls. As individuals, the musicians who would become known as the Beatles were on the leading edge of an entirely new generation.

They also did not have the wealth that came with later generations. None of the band could read music. None of them received formal training on their principal instruments. McCartney grew up in a musical household—his father was an accomplished trumpet player—but received lessons in piano. While their parents indulged their children's hobbies, they were hardly supportive of their chosen professional career path, preferring they take more traditional jobs with steadier pay.

While reliable macroeconomic data on income, unemployment, inflation, and other measures do not exist for 1950, some data exist for the dawn of the Beatles era and provides some context. While economic conditions had improved after the war, income per person in the UK lagged behind the US while the Fab Four were growing up. The UK had started out the twentieth century as the world's wealthiest nation. By 1960, however, its national income per person was less than half that of the United States according to the World Bank's World Development Indicators. (Figures for Germany are not available.) Other nations suffered worse. Japan, on the losing side of World War II, was also one of the most industrialized nations in the world and the dominant economy in Asia. Fifteen years after the war, Japan's national income per person was just $479, about 35 percent of the UK and 16 percent of the US level. Those familiar with recent economic history know that Japan's growth in the 1960s and 1970s rebounded, allowing it to regain its status as a wealthy, high-income nation. Nevertheless, the data make the point: Except for the US, the industrialized world was devastated by the war. This context is important for understanding the environment in which John Lennon, Paul McCartney, George Harrison, and Ringo Starr lived and the opportunities, commercial and artistic, that emerged around them.

Notably, Lennon, McCartney, Harrison, and Starr were born a few years prior to the beginning of the so-called Baby Boom (which generally is given the starting point of 1946). Rather, they were on the tail end of the so-called "Silent Generation," a smaller cohort that grew to adulthood in the newly prosperous 1950s and 1960s. Too young to experience the worst of the Great Depression and World War II, the generation was too old to grow up during the worst parts of the cultural upheaval of the late 1960s and 1970s. Florida State University Sociologist Elwood Carlson has called this generation "The Lucky Few" because of its ability to benefit from the rising incomes and relative social calm of this period. The Beatles rode the tail end of the Silent Generation wave while tagging onto the momentum of the next wave of Baby Boomers.

As Chapter 4 discusses more fully, the serendipity of birth had profound implications for their careers as musicians as well as popular music. While detailed data on teenage employment and growth are not available for much of Europe, what would become the epicenter of the revolution in pop culture, US trends provide some insight into this phenomenon. A decade of economic depression and the effects of World War II contributed to a stable cohort of pre-teens and teenage youth (10- to 14-year-olds) numbering about 12 million throughout the 1930s and 1940s according to the US Bureau of Labor Statistics. In 1950, the trend ticks up—dramatically. By 1960, the beginning of the Beatles decade, the US population of 10- to 14-year-olds ballooned to 17 million, a 42 percent increase. By 1970, the cohort peaked at 20 million—an increase of two-thirds over the 1950 level—before starting to decline. The cohort of US 20–24 years, predictably, held steady until 1960. Then, as the 10- to 14-year-olds became 20-year-olds, the trend line spikes upward, rising to 20 million young adults in 1980.

Thus, the Beatles hit the popular music scene at almost the perfect time: They were old enough to be a producer of entertainment that hit the sweet spot of the post-World War II Baby Boom. Beatlemania reflected the unprecedented growth in a targeted consumer population (teenagers), combined with a dramatic increase in wealth that accompanied the peace-time economy (to some extent also juiced by the Cold War). In fact, the UK's per capita income increased by 70 percent in the 1960s alone! At the same time, discretionary income, particularly among American teenagers, was increasing as more entered the workforce. Teenage (16- to 19-year-old) employment increased from 4 million in 1955 to 8 million in 1973, according to the US Bureau of Labor Statistics.

In sum, several macroeconomic trends were fundamental, perhaps even necessary conditions for Beatlemania. A growing consumer base is essential for any industry, let alone business, to survive and grow. But the consumers also need disposable income to spend on new products and services. In the case of rock music, an emergent genre imported from the US, growing income and spending had to be channeled into a new market. In short, wealth creation had to rise to the level that the incremental rise in household income could be diverted into new areas. The wealth had to be monetized through higher wages that could then be spent on niche products in new markets, like rock and roll music. These trends clearly created an economic wave for the Beatles to ride.

Is macroeconomics enough?

These trends, while favorable, are not sufficient to explain the Beatles phenomenon. Other bands, such as the Rolling Stones and the Beach Boys, also rode the economic wave at the same time but faltered. Despite touring longer and achieving moments of creative brilliance, their influence (as well as the Who, Led Zeppelin, Pink Floyd, and others) did not have the same impact on the industry. The Beatles, recording albums over a six-year period, have generated 280 million certified units based on data provided on Wikipedia's "List of Best-Selling Music Artists" (accessed October 14, 2019). They have sold significantly more than their contemporaries who were active over much longer periods of time, including Elvis Presley (224 million units), and still active bands from the British Invasion such as Led Zeppelin (140 million units), Pink Floyd (121 million units), and the Rolling Stones (99.3 million certified units).

As individuals and a band, the Beatles also had to overcome a number of barriers, some economic and some attitudinal. The list of hurdles is quite impressive. They were outside the music mainstream, building a following from working-class Liverpool with a brand marked by unusual accents. At the time, most commercial music production was centered in London, and the industry held music and musicians from the north in low regard. The Beatles also had a rough image that rubbed against the polished styles of leading R&B and rock artists such as Little Richard, Chuck Berry, Elvis Presley, the Everly Brothers, and Buddy Holly.

While the Beatles gained some notoriety in the unique blend of American folk, R&B, and blues that became known as "skiffle" and its more enduring musical progeny Merseybeat (referring to the Mersey River flowing through Manchester, Liverpool, and emptying into Liverpool Bay), the Beatles were neither the most popular band or best known. Other competitors included Rory Storm and the Hurricanes, Lonnie Donegan, Gerry and the Pacemakers, and the Merseybeats. Most of these bands, including the Beatles, earned their income as cover bands, not performing original songs. Indeed, Rory Storm and the Hurricanes was an up-and-coming band that included a rock-steady drummer named Ringo Starr. For the Beatles to survive, they had to become more than better than the other bands. They would have to fashion a professional trajectory that could attract the highest-quality talent to their band.

How did the Beatles accomplish this? Surprisingly, economics provides some insight. The next chapter discusses their origins in Liverpool and how this formative experience created an entrepreneurial spirit that allowed them to break through barriers to their success. Chapter 3 uses leading-edge theories of entrepreneurship and organizations to understand their innovation process, a critical element to establishing their enduring legacy. Chapter 4 dives deeper into how the economic system of markets created the platform that allowed their artistry to be monetized and then invested in radically new ways of creating and producing pop music. Chapter 5 takes an even deeper dive into the forces that kept the band together and, eventually, to its break-up, drawing some surprising conclusions. Chapter 6 explores why other bands failed to achieve the same success, focusing more specifically on the cases of the Rolling Stones and the Beach Boys. Chapter 7 concludes with thoughts on the Beatles legacy, the benefits of economic analysis, and some speculation on the future of pop music.

References

Bragg, Billy. 2017. *Roots, Radicals and Rockers: How Skiffle Changed the World.* London: Faber & Faber.

Carlson, Elwood. 2008. *The Lucky Few: Between the Greatest Generation and the Baby Boom.* Berlin: Springer.

Taleb, Nassim Nicholas. 2010. *The Black Swan,* 2nd edition. New York: Random House.

US Bureau of Labor Statistics. 1980. *Profile of the Teenage Worker.* Bulletin 2039, October. Washington, DC: US Department of Labor.

US Census Bureau. 2002. *Demographic Trends of the 20th Century.* November. Washington, DC: US Census Bureau.

2

LIVERPOOL START-UP

Economic concepts: Human capital, labor economics, capital theory, labor specialization, leadership, organizational culture, start-up entrepreneurship, start-up culture, venture capital

One of the more impressive observations when hearing audio recordings of the Beatles during their Hamburg "residencies" is the energy they exude on stage. Despite the low-quality recordings that have survived, their rock beat carries a power that incites the audience. The banter between the bandmates showcases an ease with each other that is also endearing. Even without video, listeners can visualize how the live audiences must have felt about the four Liverpudlians, or "Scousers," how they interacted with each other, the joy they felt on stage, and how they committed to their art. Malcolm Gladwell famously spotlighted the Beatles in his book *Outliers: The Story of Success*, when he pointed out that the band invested thousands of hours in honing their skills in live performances in Hamburg, Germany, mastering their instruments and sound before making it big in the UK and securing a coveted record contract. Economists would say they were "investing" in their "human" capital the talents and skills embedded in the people who produce products and services in a firm.

The Hamburg residencies, however, while perhaps most well known among Beatles fans, may not have been their most important formative experiences. By the time the Hamburg gigs arrived, the band had already established the rough aesthetics of their sound and as well as their musical ambitions. As a band, they were already set on becoming successful. They had abandoned conventional jobs. They had already cast aside the skepticism of family and friends to pursue their passion. The heart and soul of the band was forged in the post-war music scene in Liverpool, England.

Skiffle start-up

Liverpool has a storied history in England for reasons that have nothing to do with the Beatles. At least directly. The city played a critical role in the world's first truly sustainable industrial revolution, an economic phenomenon that started in England around the mid-seventeenth century and quickly spread to western Europe and America. As English political institutions accommodated and supported commerce, an agricultural revolution released labor from the fields and plains of the countryside to the cities. As productively increased and markets spread, incomes also rose, increasing the demand for consumer goods such as clothing and shoes. The ability to foster technical innovation through manufacturing, combined with urban labor, led to dramatic cost reductions in consumer goods, which in turn fueled higher incomes from wages in factories and mining. The ramifications of this revolution are still being felt in countries experiencing their own cycle of manufacturing-based economic revolutions, particularly in Asia.

Liverpool played a critical role in England's industrial revolution because its port emerged as a primary eighteenth-century trading center for cotton, textiles, sugar, and Indian spices. At one point, the port of Liverpool was the single largest source of revenue for the English government through customs taxes and fees. Liverpool was the site of the first commercial "wet dock" (1715) and a terminus for the first commercial railway (1830). More soberly, Liverpool was also a major part of the Atlantic slave trade, becoming a central location for eighteenth-century human trafficking as cotton from the American South became a staple input for English textiles.

Ironically, the vast expanse of the British Empire meant that men and women of a variety of races and ethnicities emigrated to Liverpool to take advantage of the economic opportunities the port provided. Ethnic and racial tensions reached a boiling point in the immediate aftermath of World War I when race riots broke out across England (and the US). The economic hardships bestowed on a nation ravaged by war, compounded by a decade-long economic slump (called the Great Depression in the US), led to massive public investments in housing. These "council houses" became an essential rung in England's housing ladder as working-class and lower-middle-income families scrambled for economic security and stability.

On one level, Liverpool would seem like an odd place to launch a pop cultural revolution. But digging a little deeper reveals a cauldron of diversity decidedly outside the mainstream of British society but fitting of the region's iconic Scouse stew. The Beatles themselves are illustrative of this diversity. John Lennon was an angry, rough teenager. Given up by his mother and merchant seaman father at a young age, he grew up with his stern and proper Aunt Mimi. His mother stayed in his life, but Lennon grew up primarily in Mimi's more stable, middle-class household. The heartache of abandonment was compounded by the trauma of the tragic loss of his mother, Julia, when she was killed in a car accident when Lennon was just seventeen.

Lennon pictured himself as Teddy Boy. While "Teds" or "Teddies" were part of a uniquely British fashion trend among teenagers that began during the 1950s, in many places they were associated with teenage rebellion and at times became violent. Lennon, by way of dress and his acerbic attitude, identified with the Teddies as a teenager. Indeed, Paul McCartney remembers getting on the bus to school fearing that the older Lennon might rough him up if he looked at him crossways. Lennon cultivated the image and was known for drinking, smoking, and being unruly in class as well as prone to fighting.

McCartney, for his part, grew up in a council house with his musically oriented father. Their family steadily advanced in socioeconomic standing over the years, but did not attain the middle-class lifestyle that privileged John Lennon while he was a teenager. To be sure, the McCartneys were not on the brink of homelessness. His father had a steady job. But Paul's upbringing was stable with loving parents. Notably, McCartney's mother, Mary, passed away from breast cancer in 1956 when he was just fourteen. Thus personal hardship was no stranger to the McCartney household. This heartache would eventually help bond him with John Lennon and inspire the lyrics to one of the most enduring songs in modern popular music, "Let It Be."

George Harrison, the youngest of the Beatles, grew up not far from either Lennon or McCartney. In fact, Harrison was a schoolmate of McCartney's. McCartney was the one who introduced Harrison to Lennon and encouraged him to invite the young guitarist into his skiffle band, the Quarrymen. Harrison's father worked on a public transit bus and on passenger ships while his mother worked in retail. He was the youngest of four children (with a sister and two brothers) and showed a keen interest in guitars at an early age. His father bought him a guitar, and he formed his own skiffle group with his brothers before meeting Paul McCartney on a bus to school (to the Liverpool Institute). Notably, Harrison showed little interest in formal schooling, acting out and failing to keep up with his school work (although he performed well enough to be promoted). He developed a focus and passion for the guitar, and quickly learned the instrument well enough to impress older boys (including McCartney).

Richard Starkey, aka Ringo Starr, in contrast, grew up in a single household as the only child of a mother who doted on him. To make ends meet, his mother cleaned houses and worked as a barmaid. At six years old, a routine appendectomy led to severe illness and a coma that lasted several days. After a year of recovery, he fell behind in his education. His failure to obtain basic competencies in reading and mathematics isolated him at school, leading to truancy. When tutoring brought him back up to speed, he contracted tuberculosis, which kept him in the hospital for another two years.

His interest in percussion began while he was in the hospital with tuberculosis. The nursing staff had created a make-shift toy that he quickly turned into a stick he could use to drum. His passion for drums started there, and kept him focused, but he never recovered from the interruptions to his studies caused by his childhood illnesses. At fifteen, Starkey left school and shuffled around from job to job, including stints with British Rail, a waiter, and as a machinist's apprentice. Starkey was introduced to skiffle music while working at an equipment manufacturing company. He eventually paired up with friends to form the Eddie Miles Band. As his drumming skills (and variety of percussion equipment) expanded, he moved up through the ranks of the skiffle scene. He adopted the stage name of Ringo Starr after joining Rory Storm and the Hurricanes, one of the best-known and most successful of the Liverpool skiffle bands.

Importantly, none of the Beatles had the privilege of formal musical education. Julia Lennon introduced John to the music of emergent rock and rollers such as Elvis Presley and jazz greats such as Fats Domino, and she bought John his first guitar. But his Aunt Mimi, with whom he lived, famously told him "the guitar's all well and good, John, but you'll never make a living out of it." Paul McCartney's father wanted him to learn an instrument that would allow him to find a steady job. His preference was piano. But young Paul never connected to the instrument, preferring the electric guitar. Of the four, Harrison had the most support. He took to the guitar at an early age, and his mother supported his musical interests. He father reluctantly bought him a guitar, but didn't discourage him. These skills would become critical to Harrison's acceptance into the Quarrymen.

Rock and roll was also in its infancy during the 1950s as the genre struggled to break out from the more established styles such as country, jazz, and blues. The genre was not well enough established and many mainstream promoters were unwilling to take the risk necessary to invest in bands without more knowledge of the market. Rock and roll, for many, was still a fad with a narrow economic base. The disposable income that was fueling the rise of the teenage consumer market was still in the making. England and Europe were willing to headline major US-based jazz and blues musicians. While band members were often fluid, most successful bands had well-defined and recognized front men who led the group and its branding. Buddy Holly and the Crickets ranked among the more influential acts for the Beatles, but other influences included Carl Perkins, Elvis Presley, Chuck Berry, Little Richard, and Roy Orbison. Local bands branded themselves in similar ways and included Rory Storm and the Hurricanes and Gerry and the Pacemakers.

Northern England, as music producer George Martin would point out, was hardly considered the leading edge of popular music. The cultural and economic center of England was London, not the bombed-out cities and outlying towns of the nation's manufacturing and mining belt. While concert promoting could fill music halls, theaters, and ballrooms, many of these tours had multiple bands rounding out the ticket with one headliner. While the Beatles were increasingly making a name for themselves, as late as winter 1963 they were still not the primary draw. When they toured with English jazz singer Helen Shapiro, they were fourth among eleven acts on the program. (Beatlemania, however, was just getting off the ground, and the Beatles would end up sharing the top billing with Roy Orbison during their third national tour later in May and June.)

Complicating matters for the Beatles and other England-bred rock and roll bands was the "skiffle" craze. Skiffle was a uniquely British subgenre of live performance music that borrowed from folk, country, R&B, and an emergent rock genre. The movement was profoundly important to the development of British rock, and laid critical foundation stones for what would become the so-called "British invasion" of rock and roll in America. The music engaged teenagers through its fast pace and hard edge, drawing direct inspiration from the rising rock scene in North American, but created its own set of rock stars. Rock music historian Billy Bragg pegs the "genesis" of the skiffle craze to July 1954 when Lonnie Donegan recorded and released "Rock Island Line." Skiffle fundamentally changed the pop music landscape, but most music industry elites believed it was a craze. Its rough, amateurish sound gave little indication that the bands could rise above their humble origins to have long-term impact. For the most part, they were right.

Thus, as the 1950s unfolded, the personal, social, and economic environment in which the Beatles were playing was hardly a harbinger of future success. Lennon, Harrison, and Starr had opted out of traditional education as a pathway toward economic security. McCartney had passed enough of his exams to move on, but chose to stay in pop music. Their families were less than enthusiastic about their career choices. Northern England was considered a musical backwater, and the groups coming up were tarnished with the amateurish reputation of skiffle. Few had yet grasped the implications of the growing economic power of teenagers and how they would transform the entertainment marketplace for entertainment. Few would even consider banking on four scruffy working-class boys from Liverpool. What they could not see, however, was how Liverpool would shape and forge the worldview and commitment that would become the core of the Beatles.

Skiffle's basic musical structure and pared-down band ensemble—a guitar, vocalist, upright box bass, and snare drum—allowed kids from modest economic backgrounds to acquire the instruments necessary to perform. Experience with the instruments and formal knowledge of music was optional. The bands often played for free, trying to stand out in a very crowded field. But skiffle also met an important need as teenagers emerged from the shadows of their parents to craft their own popular music culture.

In economic terms, the pop music market in Liverpool was highly competitive with more than 300 skiffle groups competing against each other. Musicians with varying levels of talent and aptitude flowed in and out of these bands. Most, like George Harrison's, were bands started by brothers and close friends, coming and going as quickly as the relationships. The barriers to entry, economists would say, were extremely low. John Lennon started several skiffle bands, but that one that seemed to stick was called the Quarrymen. The name was taken from Quarry Bank School (the equivalent of an American high school).

While skiffle had petered out by the end of the 1950s, the fad created an untethered environment for kids to test new sounds, learn new instruments, and sharpen their performance skills. Some, such as Rory Storm and the Hurricanes and Gerry and the Pacemakers, became local celebrities and toured clubs and camps throughout Great Britain. The Quarrymen, for the most part, struggled to find their own spot, playing in the shadows of the more established bands. Nevertheless, Liverpool had created what we would now call "start-up culture" around skiffle. This genre would eventually evolve into the more enduring signature sound of Merseybeat and beat music in the 1960s.

Human capital and the firing of Pete Best

Given the low barriers to entry, the general lack of talent, and low (or no) compensation levels, bands struggled to stay together as their members chose school, work, or the military as an alternative to the hapless life of wayward musicians. Lennon struggled to keep the Quarrymen together. Adding Paul McCartney was a significant step forward. McCartney was an overall better musician and found it naturally easier to pick up instruments. He was also ambitious with an eye toward organization and marketing. McCartney wanted to make it big and, more so than Lennon, had a mind that understood the business end of their profession. He also could spot talent. Even though George Harrison was younger than any of the bandmates, he was a better guitar player (and Paul McCartney was a better player than Lennon). McCartney introduced Harrison to Lennon and relentlessly urged him to add him into the line-up. On a more controversial note, McCartney also understood that Pete Best, a Beatles mainstay and drummer prior to Ringo Starr (in 1960–1962), was mediocre. By many accounts, including Best, McCartney tried to oust him and replace him with someone else.

Best's drumming fell well below what would be necessary to elevate the Beatles to a national stage. From an economic perspective, this is an important reminder that human capital is not simply a linear accumulation of skills, drive, and ambition. Talent and innate knowledge also counts. Both Brian Epstein, the Beatles manager, and George Martin, their producer at Parlophone Records, recognized that Best was a liability for the band. Indeed, the effects of Best's subpar abilities and the implications for the other three to judge talent lingered beyond his firing. Questions about Best's abilities factored into later decisions by Martin to sideline his successor, Ringo Starr, during their first recording sessions.

Pete Best, however, had two important elements running in his favor in the early years of the band. First, the Beatles did not have an alternative. Drummers were hard to come by in Liverpool, in part because drums were relatively expensive instruments. Without a steady income or the potential to earn income, other bands were able to compete more effectively for percussionists. The labor market for drummers, in economics jargon, was "thin" even though the market for skiffle bands was "thick."

A second factor, however, more than balanced out their drummer's lack of talent. Pete Best's mother, Mona Best, was committed to the band and created a venue in which to play. Their first regular venue was in the family basement, which had been converted into a nightclub called the Casbah Coffee Club. From here, Mona Best created a platform for the band that could then be supplemented by performances at better known venues, such as the now famous Cavern Club. This familial entanglement would become a stumbling block when the band recognized it would need to fire Pete in order for the band to move to the next level.

Nevertheless, this relationship also points to the importance of platforms for artists as they hone their skills and build a customer base. While the firing of Best is still controversial, and different accounts and memories cannot seem to reconcile the details, a new drummer was clearly in the cards for the band to work. Later, McCartney remarked about the first time Ringo Starr played with the band. Starr was touring with Rory Storm and the Hurricanes at the time. He would often watch the Beatles play, and occasionally subbed for a missing Pete Best during their gigs. McCartney recalls listening to Starr's drumming, most likely his signature steady beat, and nodding to John Lennon during the performance affirming a mutually recognized difference in the quality of the drumming. The writing was on the wall. Having the right people and talent on the team was critical for the Beatles to make it. The only question was when the decision to let their drummer go would be.

Firing Pete Best came with significant economic risks. In addition to potentially losing their most steady playing venue, the Beatles had an enthusiastic fan base. Lines would extend around the block of the Cavern Club when they played despite its dank, foreboding basement interior. Condensation dripped down the walls from the heat of bodies, making some marvel at how no one was electrocuted during their performances. At one point, producer George Martin recalls a teenage girl toward the front of the stage fainted and had to be extracted by fans passing her unconscious body over their heads to the exit. Pete Best was an integral component of developing the Beatles' fan base. He was widely recognized as the most attractive member and had become an important element of the band's look and marketing image. When Best was fired, enraged fans scuffled with the remaining members of the band as they arrived for one of their gigs at the Cavern Club. George Harrison ended up taking the stage with a black eye.

Fortunately for Pete Best, the thin market for drummers meant that he could find another band to play with although they never rose to prominence. Pete's mother also took the high road and did not throw the Beatles to the curb. The band was still enough of a draw that the economic health of the club superseded her personal disappointment. The Beatles' road manager, Neil Aspinall, who was also Pete Best's close friend, also remained with the band.

While Pete Best's firing was personally crushing, and not decided upon lightly, the episode is an important reminder that the bandmates recognized that friendship had its limits in the music business. In order for the Beatles to achieve their ambitions, they needed the best talent possible. But musical talent was only part of the story. They also needed to have the right people on the team in order to create the value they needed to stand out in a very competitive market.

Notably, none of the major recording studios in London believed that rock music had long-term potential. They believed, like skiffle, it was a fad and would fade away. Moreover, none of the recording studios had taken a risk on a band or popular music artists from "the North." While the Beatles desperately wanted a recording contract, and rightly understood it would be critical for their long-term success, they also knew their success would only come if they had the right band. Much later in life, Paul McCartney was asked if they could have been as successful if they had different members. His response was no. The Beatles had to be the four that made it. He was probably right (as Chapter 3 discusses). They also recognized they could not do it alone.

Hamburg and the forging of a brand

For many, the Beatles did not appear on the pop music scene until they started their "residencies" in Hamburg, Germany. These gigs, typically consisting of six- and eight-hour performances, were more of a transition point than a terminus. Human capital is rarely acquired all at once. Learning, proficiency, and skill development is an ongoing process. Thus, the Hamburg residencies should be viewed along a continuum of learning and knowledge accumulation. Moreover, the trajectory of their talent development was not necessarily linear. In fact, the Hamburg residencies may well be considered an inflection point along a curve that found the rate of human capital accumulating at an increasing rate after leaving Liverpool. Whereas the skiffle bands, the Casbah Coffee Club, and other venues provided a performance-based foundation for their musical abilities, Hamburg allowed each of the Beatles to become skilled musicians and see the benefits of working as a band—the group's success was bigger than the sum of its parts. Residencies, combined with touring, allowed the members to develop the intimate knowledge they needed to form a cohesive team. In economics jargon, they formed a "firm," or an organization with the dedicated mission of producing a service for public consumption—rock and roll music.

Their booking agent, Allan Williams, recognized that their future success (and their ability to earn revenue) depended on their ability to improve their musi- cianship and broaden their fan base. In terms of the scale and productivity of their enterprise, the Beatles had gone about as far as they could go as a local band in Liverpool. A multi-week engagement outside Britain would validate them as artists and give them time to hone their skills. In 1960, Williams contracted the Beatles for a "residency" in Hamburg, Germany.

The clubs where the band would play—the Indra Club, Kaiserkeller, and Top Ten Club—were hardly upscale. They were concentrated in Hamburg's raucous and irre- verent "red light" district, populated by prostitutes, gangsters, and rough sorts of all types. The Beatles were chagrined to learn that their first gigs (in the Indra Club) were not in the best venue. They learned the better bands were booked into the higher- paying Kaiserkeller and Top Ten Club. They also were also forced to live in rooms that were former storerooms, backed up to the bathrooms, and without adequate plumbing or other utilities. Nevertheless, the venues had status outside of Britain, and they paid the musicians well enough they could give up their "day" jobs.

They played long hours—getting in the famous "ten thousand hours" of intensive practice that psychologist K. Anders Ericsson and his colleagues found essential for mastery—often starting in the afternoon and playing well into the night. And they eventually moved to the Kaiserkeller in October 1960. They then moved to the Top Ten Club because it paid better and had better audio equipment. The choice to move to the new venue, however, nearly destroyed the Beatles as a band.

Moving to the Top Ten Club involved a breach of contract with the owner of the Kaiserkeller, who then reported George Harrison to the German police for working under age. Harrison was deported in November. While motives and stories differ, Pete Best and Paul McCartney apparently started a small fire in the rooms behind the Kaiserkeller as they were retrieving personal belongings from their rooms at the old venue. This prompted the owner to report them for arson. Best and McCartney were arrested and deported in December. Lennon's work permit was revoked soon thereafter, and he was dispatched by train. (Stu Sutcliffe, their bass player at the time, stayed in London with his German girlfriend Astrid Kirchherr.) Thus, the Beatles' first residency came to an unexpected and abrupt end. Discouraged and depressed, the band remained in Liverpool out of contact with each other for several weeks before they reunited and started to play again.

Once George Harrison turned eighteen, however, the Beatles returned to Hamburg for a second and pivotal residency. This residency was arranged by their new manager, Brian Epstein, who had a plan to upgrade their image and create a marketable band built on their ever expanding fan base in northern England. The Beatles started out at the Top Ten Club this time, playing from March through July. Their living arrangements were markedly better, reflecting their better contract, living in a dorm rather than an unfinished former storeroom.

In a decision that would have profound implications for the future of pop music, Stu Sutcliffe decided to formally leave the band at this point and move in with Kirchherr full time to focus on his long-time passion for art. (Sutcliffe tragically died a short time thereafter.) The Beatles were now left without a bass player. While the Hamburg music scene allowed the Beatles to tap into all sorts of talent in an ad hoc fashion—this is how Ringo Starr became familiar with the group and its members—the bass player was a pivotal member of the band. Since John Lennon, George Harrison, and Pete Best were all uninterested in playing bass guitar, McCartney decided to try it out. (McCartney's own recollection is more flippant. He was walking past a music store in Hamburg, saw a Höfner violin bass guitar in the window, and thought it looked cool, so decided to give it a try.)

McCartney already played guitar and started to learn other instruments on his own. So picking up the bass guitar was a challenge but not an overwhelming obstacle. This entrepreneurial approach to music would serve the band well as they moved more into songwriting and continued to experiment with new sounds and song structures. Notably, McCartney did not play the bass in a conventional style, using his fingers to pluck the strings. Rather, he used (and continues to use) a guitar pick which gives the bass sound a more defined and harder edge. He also played according to his own musical sensibilities—melodically. McCartney's melodic bass playing would become his signature style and fundamentally change the sound of the Beatles, setting a new course for the instrument in rock music.

The band was evolving to a new level of professionalism and coherence. Their network expanded and created new opportunities for them as their musicianship developed and defined a unique sound. The second residency also gave them the opportunity to record their first song. Having met up with Tony Sheridan, they played on a cover version of the British folk classic "My Bonnie." The song was recorded in June and May 1962 and released in October by the German division of Polydor Records.

Brian Epstein was now firmly in charge as their manager, adding a business sensibility that the young musicians (except for McCartney) had yet to develop. Epstein, a second generation music store retailer in Liverpool and occasional contributor to the local pop music newspaper *Mersey Beat*, had heard of the Beatles by reputation, saw them perform in the Cavern Club in Liverpool, and immediately recognized their potential. Realizing that the extended residencies were important for their continued development as musicians and performers, he booked the second residency in the Top Ten Club, a third residency in the Star-Club (April 1962 to May 1962), and a fourth residency in the Star-Club. By the third residency, the band was earning enough that their road manager, Neil Aspinall, could make more money with the band than working as an accountant. By the fourth residency—also in the Star-Club in November and December 1962—Ringo Starr had replaced Pete Best, Epstein had secured a recording contract with Parlophone records, and the Beatles recorded their first song, "Love Me Do" (September 1962). By December, they were staying in regular hotels with single rooms for the first time. "Love Me Do" was released in October 1962 and rose to number 17 on the pop charts in the UK. (The song peaked at number one on the US charts when it was released in that country two years later in 1964.)

Underestimating the importance of the Hamburg residencies in the professional development of the Beatles as musicians and performance artists is hard. From a human capital perspective, the playing served two important purposes. As individual musicians, they afforded them the playing time and focus to improve dramatically above the amateur venues in Liverpool. As a band, the residencies allowed the individual members to develop an internal working relationship allowing for specialization and division of labor. George Harrison developed his playing skills, sensibility, and an aesthetic on lead guitar that complemented the rhythm guitar of John Lennon, bass playing of Paul McCartney, and drumming of Ringo Starr. These performances were an essential component for creating a tightness within the band that would become a foundation stone for future evolutions of the band. The constant playing also allowed them to develop a rapport with their audience that allowed them to convert them from listeners to fans, an effect that became evident once they began their national concert tours in 1963.

Hamburg itself was not homogeneous. The entertainment scene was a rough-and-tumble place, with its own hierarchy of talent and respect that required the

Beatles to pay their dues. The industrial city's red light district was known more for its strip clubs, heavy drug and alcohol abuse, and prostitution, than the finer points of music. But this is what the Beatles needed, and their managers, Allan Williams and then Brian Epstein, knew it. When the Beatles started at the Indra Club during their first residency, they were not the headline act. Rory Storm and the Hurricanes were a much bigger name and draw. Their performances, however, would often end in the early morning hours of the next day, meaning they would find themselves in bed by late morning, sleeping into the afternoon.

In Hamburg, the Beatles were hard, dedicated workers. Much of their off-stage behavior in Hamburg reflected their youth. As young men in their teens, they certainly took advantage of the untamed nature of the city. Their sexual and drinking exploits during the Hamburg years are well known and recognized. In the misogynistic male-dominated culture of the late 1950s, girlfriends left behind in Liverpool were soon forgotten, at least in terms of recreation. By at least one account, each of the Beatles contracted STDs. Nevertheless, Lennon and McCartney both returned to their steady girlfriends after their residencies. Lennon, in fact, married his long-time girlfriend Cynthia when she became pregnant with his oldest son Julian. But the Beatles also worked hard, honing their skills on their instruments as they played covers of the most popular American and European R&B and rock songs.

Fortunately, some audio tapes of the Beatles performances toward the end of their Hamburg residencies survived and were eventually released on vinyl in 1977 (many of the recordings are also available on YouTube). While the songs represent the coalescence of their own sound, the comradery of the band is also evident. When one of the bandmates makes a mistake, for example, they can be heard giggling and laughing through the rough parts. Occasionally, they forget the lyrics of the song they are using. In between songs, Lennon's acerbic wit is evident as he engages in deprecating banter with the audience. Their performances are also energetic as they put a slightly faster pace and accent onto the music. These artistic touches would become part of the band's signature sound that would ignite a rabidly loyal and enthusiastic fan base. In effect, these elements became part of their brand and, when more polished and professional, became a core component of what endeared the bandmates to their supporters.

Brian Epstein as venture capitalist

As important as the residencies were, their impact would have been muted if the band hadn't returned to the UK and continue playing in Liverpool. Epstein certainly understood the marketing value of their first paid performances. Upon their return, flyers at their venues advertised their return from Hamburg as a way to ramp up the band's visibility. The Beatles reputation continued to grow as their consumer base grew. Epstein also intentionally fashioned an image to replace the black leather, rebellious image the Beatles courted in Hamburg with a cleaner, more cohesive brand projected by suits and a clean-cut grooming. But the end game was never to become the most popular band in Liverpool. Rather the goal was to land a recording contract and become commercially successful.

Epstein was more than a manager. He was also a venture capitalist. He invested his own funds and talent in the band with the hopes it would take off and provide the foundation for a much larger pop music enterprise. With the band's popularity growing and its fan base expanding and deepening, Epstein financed demo tapes he shopped to different recording studios in London, the epicenter for music in the UK (and a gateway to the Continental European and American markets). The Beatles were not a slam dunk. As George Martin (the producer at EMI/Parlophone Records who "discovered" them) notes, the music industry was stuck in older genres. They didn't think musicians from the north would be able to compete effectively, and they thought popular music lacked the staying power to generate substantial revenues.

Ironically, but perhaps not coincidentally, a Peter Sellers comedy show produced by George Martin on Parlophone was one of the reasons the Beatles were excited to sign with the label. Parlophone Records was best known for its comedy recordings such as *The Goon Show*, which featured the surreal comedy of Sellers along with Spike Milligan and Harry Secombe. Martin was given the reins to the studio mainly because it was the smallest and least valuable property in the suite of recording companies owned by EMI. The off-beat humor connected with all members of the Beatles, who were fans and listened regularly (and later provided the creative framework for their movies *A Hard Day's Night* and *Help!*).

In retrospect, Martin's signing of the Beatles must be registered as one of the greatest business decisions in music history. But the decision carried significant risk. Parlophone was the last label Epstein approached to sign the Beatles after being turned down by all the others. Martin, for his part, saw some potential in the Liverpudlians even though he recognized their music was raw and needed polish. Despite being a classically trained musician and student, history shows that Martin had a keen sense of what popular culture would support commercially. Even Martin held back at first. The Beatles had to audition in the studio. The contract came after the audition and was limited in scope.

Managing the human capital

Artisanship and creativity are just two elements of building a cultural enterprise. To be sustainable and successful, the Beatles also needed someone with a business background who could manage them and take them to a new level of professional success. This was a critical function for Brian Epstein, and he invested more with greater success than previous managers, such as Allan Williams, who saw their roles in a more narrow way. Epstein would not just book their shows. He would build a brand and market them to a global audience.

Epstein had heard of the Beatles as their consumer base started to grow in Liverpool. Their performances from the basement pub Casbah and the Cavern Club reflected their success as they broke out of the skiffle craze and established themselves as a contemporary rock and R&B band. As the owner and proprietor of one of Liverpool's most successful music shops, NEMS music store, he also noted their rising popularity as teens and young adults would come into his store asking for records (which did not exist). Their popularity had prompted him to buy 25 copies of the record they had produced with Tony Sheridan. When he saw the Beatles play at the Cavern Club, his business intuition and acumen merged. He saw the raw ingredients of a band that could become much bigger and commercially successful. On November 9, 1961, he had lunch with the Beatles at the Cavern Club and a business partnership was forged.

By the time Epstein signed with the Beatles, they were already a hot property in Liverpool. The marketing benefits of their Hamburg residencies gave them bragging rights among the hundreds of bands competing for the attention of the market. They were crowned the most popular group hailing from Merseyside in January 1962 based on a poll conducted by *Mersey Beat* magazine and the Cavern Club's popular DJ, Bob Wooler (who gave the Beatles lots of play with their record produced with Tony Sheridan in Hamburg).

In retrospect, the Beatles recognized they knew very little about contracts, and the business side of popular music. They were fortunate in that Epstein was an honorable businessman. In fact, he came to see himself as a father figure for the band as he guided them up the rungs toward commercial success. Epstein recognized that the band needed several improvements before it would be commercially successful. They had, in entrepreneurship terms, demonstrated an MVP—minimum viable product—but not established its mass appeal. Epstein rightfully recognized the value in the essential product—a rock edge to R&B built on American popular music—and worked with them to improve the design. Before he could secure a record contract, and a shot at commercial success, they needed to hone their music. They also needed to rebrand themselves for the broader market.

Economic implications

The story of the Beatles, then, provides important insight into three critical elements of economic analysis: human capital, entrepreneurial start-ups, and venture capital. Liverpool was a hotbed of a unique pop music culture, breeding hundreds of amateur bands. These bands became an important source of human capital development, as some musicians gave up on their dreams and others persevered to make their own name and place in the music scene. Still others failed because they could not develop the competencies and skill sets needed to become cornerstones of a dynamic and fast-evolving music culture.

The individual Beatles—John Lennon, Paul McCartney, George Harrison, and Ringo Starr—were not stand out talents or identified as being uniquely qualified skiffle or rock artists. Quite the contrary, they slogged through the scene, but persevered. They experienced nominal success within Liverpool's innovative pop music start-up culture. The music blended teenage angst with rising incomes, and an optimism that helped lift Europe from the apocalyptic aftermath of World War

II. As the early 1960s unfolded, their potential to be more than a local celebrity was evident. But optimism, commitment, and young-adult idealism were not enough to take the Beatles to the next level. They needed entrepreneurial partners with expertise and knowledge in other aspects of the industry to give them a shot at commercial success. These partners came in the form of Brian Epstein on the business side and George Martin on the artistic side.

But what can economics add to the discussion of artisanship and creativity? More than you might think, particularly through the lens of cutting-edge ideas on how firms form, why they dissolve, and how they operate internally. The next chapter provides a deeper dive into these issues using the framework of economic analysis.

References

Bragg, Billy. 2017. *Roots, Radicals and Rockers: How Skiffle Changed the World*. London: Faber & Faber.

Gladwell, Malcom. 2008. *Outliers: The Story of Success*. New York: Little Brown and Company.

Lewison, Mark. 2013. *Tune In: The Beatles: All These Years, Vol. 1*. New York: Three Rivers Press.

Martin, George. 1994. *All You Need Is Ears: The Inside Personal Story of the Genius Who Created the Beatles*. New York: St. Martin's Griffin.

Norman, Philip. 2003. *Shout! The Beatles in Their Generation*, revised edition. New York: Fireside Books.

Norman, Philip. 2016. *Paul McCartney: The Life*. New York: Little Brown and Company.

3

INNOVATION, ENTREPRENEURSHIP, AND THE GROWTH MINDSET

Economic concepts: Transaction costs, principal–agent theory, growth mindset, innovation, entrepreneurship, risk, uncertainty, strategic judgement, organizational behavior

The Beatles' contribution to popular music is dizzying. They recorded over 200 songs in the studio over an eight-year period, covered scores of songs by other artists live on stage and radio, and made unique contributions to more than 60 genres and subgenres of music. The bandmates were early adopters of new technology, borrowed liberally from other artists for inspiration for their own music, and supported continuous innovation and experimentation throughout their decade-long career.

Moreover, many of their songs contributed to multiple genres. "Love Me Do," their first hit record in Britain, has been tagged as an example of the distinctive Liverpudlian sound of Merseybeat, rock and roll, rhythm and blues (R&B), and pop. Fans and experts have credited "Tomorrow Never Knows," a track off the path-breaking *Revolver* album, with contributing to psychedelic rock, avant-garde, electronic music, and raga (Indian) pop. The subgenre of electronic music is particularly interesting because the song represents ground-breaking experimentation in the studio with revolutionary techniques such as tape loops, backwards guitar recording, unconventional drumming, and creative use of speakers to project vocals even though the band and recording engineers did not yet have access to electronic instruments such as synthesizers (which were used later on *Abbey Road*). The Beatles music contributed to the establishment or mainstreaming of numerous new genres and subgenres of popular rock music. Overall, recorded Beatles songs have been tagged 325 times with one of more than 60 genres and subgenres based on a review of the open-source online website Wikipedia. While not definitive, Wikipedia captures a broad range of popular and artistic reactions to the Beatles and other bands. Thus, it serves as a reasonable indicator of the band's influence in popular culture.

While a word cloud reveals one genre stood out among their songs recorded in the studio—the general category of "rock"—dozens of other genres also took a front seat in their recording (Figure 3.1). The Beatles engaged in a wide range of experiments in the style, song structure, and composition of popular music. Some genres were more prominent than others, but the band was willing to deviate significantly from the mainstream as well as cross over into other genres. Thus, their body of work includes dozens of hyphenated sub-genres which reflected their willingness to poach from other styles for inspiration. Thus, they contributed to folk rock, baroque, psychedelic rock, psychedelic pop, music hall, electronic art rock, orchestral skiffle among dozens of others.

This experimentation is a signature element of their creative process. Their innovation, however, was not a signature element of mainstream popular music. Even the most influential artists often stayed in their "lane," innovating within their genre rather than broadening the expanse and territory of popular music more generally. The Beatles did more than innovate within their initial genre—rock and roll, Merseybeat, skiffle—they radically expanded the frontiers of popular music generally. How they achieved this feat is the subject of this chapter.

FIGURE 3.1 Word cloud of genres and subgenres represented in the Beatles' released studio recordings

Source: Created by the author from Wikipedia, "List of Songs Recorded by the Beatles," last accessed by author June 25, 2019

Liverpudlian foundation stones for innovation

Rock music, particularly the music that grounded the early years of Rock and Roll, was foundational to the development of the Beatles' sound and, in many ways, defined the development of popular music for the next several generations. In fact, the rock foundation never completely retreated from the Beatles catalogue. While the early years included covers of "Roll Over Beethoven" (Chuck Berry), "Twist and Shout" (made famous by the Isley Brothers), and "Boys" (made famous by the Shirelles), the Beatles quickly established their rock credentials with their first hits and album with songs such as "I Saw Her Standing There," "Love Me Do," "Please Please Me," and others. This musical interest continued well into the latter part of their career but also expanded the edges of the genre. "Helter Skelter," a song explicitly written by Paul McCartney as a hard driving, grinding rock song, is considered a key contribution to what is now called "heavy metal" and even inspired the aggressive sound of punk in the 1970s. In fact, McCartney said he tackled the song in response to a release from the Who, which he thought wasn't "hard" enough. Songs such as "Day Tripper," "Hey Bulldog," "Revolution," and "I Want You/She's So Heavy" are also considered part of the canon of the hard rock sound.

At the same time the band's baroque contributions mainstreamed the use of, with the influence of gifted producer George Martin, orchestral arrangements that defined the genre of baroque pop. "Yesterday" was the first pop rock song to include an orchestra (an eight-piece string section) and is widely considered one of the most widely covered songs and perhaps the most covered Beatles song (with over 2,200 known cover versions). "Hey Jude," another classic, included a 26-piece orchestra. "In My Life" sped up the piano to sound like a harpsichord. The remarkably poignant and introspective "For No One" puts in a French horn solo by perhaps the best horn session musician in London to establish a creative and emotional touch point. "Penny Lane" has a signature piccolo trumpet that pushed the boundaries of the instrument and a world-class musician. Indeed, these songs as well as dozens of others—"Let It Be," "Blackbird," or "Here, There and Everywhere" to name a few—would be perfectly at home in a cabaret or night club. Frank Sinatra called "Something" perhaps the best love song written in the last half of the twentieth century.

These contributions raise the following question: What explains these extraordinary artistic and commercial achievements? The lens of economics helps untangle some of this mystery. New economic insights from the fields of entrepreneurship and management allow us to go inside the "black box" of the band to tease out the group and individual dynamics that probably contributed to this extraordinary and robust period of creativity and innovation. Organizational theory and the emerging field of entrepreneurial judgement provide insight into how conscious decisions, intention, and organizational culture contributed to creating and sustaining the Beatles as a creative force and commercial success.

While innate talent certainly played a critical role, it can't explain it all. The music industry is rife with talented songwriters and musicians in all genres and styles—Fats Domino (jazz), Carole King (pop), Bob Dylan and Joni Mitchell (folk), Bruce Springsteen (rock), to name just a few. Mick Jagger and Keith Richards (the Rolling Stones) certainly rivaled the Lennon/McCartney duo in rock and roll. Brian Wilson (the Beach Boys) pushed the creative boundaries of popular music as much as the Beatles. But the influence of the Beatles endured for beyond their break up, and they remain the "great among greats." (Chapter 6 revisits this question by diving deeper into the experiences and professional development of the Rolling Stones and the Beach Boys to explore this question further.)

Economics, it turns out, is an unusual but productive lens through which the creative process can be examined. Economics is a social science rooted in choice, most often rational choice. Individuals make decisions on their best estimate of which ones will create the most value. While most economists approach these choices looking through a "utilitarian" lens—based on a cold calculus of cost and benefit—another approach lends itself to recognizing value created through artistic expression. While artists may not keep a ledger of costs and benefits, they use a wide range of experience, knowledge, and calculations to determine their course of expression. Songs, for example, have certain structures. Songwriters will break down their compositions into verse, chorus, or bridge. They will layer in, often through experimentation, different textures created by instruments, voices, or other sounds to create an effect. The lyrics are crafted to complement the music.

While the final cut may not follow the rigorous scientific method typically taught in laboratories or worked through in mathematical formulas, artistic decisions are often made in a non-random way. Even without the explicit calculus, artists judge the value of what they create through their experience and connections to their work. In popular music, one of these connections is to the audience, the consumers of their art. Much of the information, knowledge or data is "tacit," or implicit, known only to the artist because of its aesthetic quality. Nevertheless, the mere fact a decision is made, and the decision is intentional—should a piccolo trumpet be added to "Penny Lane," for example, or a French horn to "For No One"?—means that understanding how these decisions are made provides insight into the creative process and whether (or how) it might be sustained. Of course, in the case of the Beatles, the process also broke down—the band split up because the "whole" could not be maintained. But that is the subject of Chapter 5. The sections below focus on the creative process and how it was sustained during their time together as a band.

Inside the black box of the Beatles

The Beatles were a band. This may seem obvious, but many discussions of the Beatles tend to focus on the most visible members—John Lennon and Paul McCartney. The contributions of George Harrison and Ringo Starr are often overlooked. Yet, when fans of the Beatles rank their favorite songs (most notably on Sirius XM's The Beatles Channel), Harrison inevitably captures three spots with "While My Guitar Gently Weeps," "Something," and "Here Comes the Sun." These songs are also ranked by artists, and even the other Beatles, as among the finest songs ever written and produced.

Ringo Starr is ignored because he wasn't a prolific songwriter. (He only wrote two that were released by the Beatles.) Yet, Starr's influence on the band was profound. His steady beat, tactical fills, intuitive feel for the music, and sense of rhythm and cadence were essential ingredients to the Beatles sound. Starr's drumming inspired numerous other musicians, many of them leading figures in contemporary rock. David Grohl (Nirvana) notes that the best drummers are the ones that "sit in the song with their own feel. Ringo was the king of feel." Taylor Hawkins (Foo Fighters) refers to the "Ringo swing" as a style on the high-hat symbols. "I wouldn't be a drummer without Ringo," says Abe Laboriel, Jr., a legendary session and touring drummer. "That is the DNA of pretty much everything I do." In Starr's Rock & Roll Hall of Fame bio, music producer Don Was says Starr "is the leading and most musical drummer to influence generations of musicians." Even in retrospect, Ringo Starr ranks as a world-class musician in his own right during his time with the Beatles.

The members of the Beatles certainly understood the importance of Starr's role in the band. John Lennon later told *Rolling Stone* in 1980 that "Ringo's talent would have come out one way or the other … whatever that spark is in Ringo, we all know it but can't put our finger on it … Ringo is a damn good drummer." Starr was inducted into the Rock & Roll Hall of Fame in 2015 as a solo act, and *Rolling Stone* magazine readers ranked him the "fifth greatest drummer of all time." *Modern Drummer* writer Robyn Flans "cannot count the number of drummers who have told me that Ringo inspired their passion for drums." Rock music reviewer columnist Steve Smith says that Starr's popularity with the Beatles "brought forth a new paradigm in how the public saw drummers. We started to see the drummer as an equal participant in the compositional aspect." Starr defined, Smith continues, "the archetype of the present-day rock drummer."

Fans, however, often gravitate toward one member, not the group as a collective. This is unfortunate, because the secret to the Beatles was, in fact, the group dynamic. George Martin may have said it best in his memoir *All You Need is Ears*. He was so "coloured" by the success of bands with individual leaders,

> I couldn't imagine a group being successful as a group. I felt that one of them was bound to come out as having a better voice than the others. Whoever that was would be the one, and the rest would become like Cliff Richard's backing group, the Shadows. I was quite wrong.

Martin put each one to the test, but what made the Beatles work was the fact they were a group. "I was thinking, on balance," he writes, "that I should make Paul the leader. Then, after some thought, I realized that if I did so I would be changing the nature of the group." Ever the entrepreneur, Martin kept the group dynamic.

His thinking was reinforced when he traveled to Liverpool and watched them perform in the Cavern Club. He saw that they had a "total commitment" to their music, and their fans (mainly teenagers) were responding enthusiastically.

Pioneering psychologist Carol S. Dweck, author of *Mindset: The New Psychology of Success*, defines the "growth mindset" as one where people believe their intelligence can be developed rather than assume it's fixed. Students who adopted the growth mindset outperformed those that did not. In effect, they could "grow their brains." Moreover, if they had mental discipline and inquisitive behaviors, they would learn and perform better. This concept has become a foundational concept underlying our current understanding of entrepreneurship.

In common language, many people think of entrepreneurs as people who own, manage, and start businesses. Indeed, many entrepreneurs do. Economists, however, think of entrepreneurs as being more than business owners. They increasingly distinguish between an entrepreneur (a noun) and entrepreneurship (a verb). Entrepreneurs are innovators who develop new products and services, often with a vision that extends beyond what current consumers may even consider. Entrepreneurship is the process of identifying market niches, new products and services, or new ways of serving customers. Entrepreneurs identify and fill "holes" in the market or, in some cases develop entirely new ones (becoming "disrupters").

In market-based economies, entrepreneurs are most often people who start up new private companies. Steve Jobs and Apple Inc. (the tech company) are one example, where the iPod radically changed how listeners consumed music as well as other audio products such as speeches, radio shows, and interviews through digital technology and Internet-based interfaces. The term "podcast" appeared in 2004 (according to the Merriam-Webster dictionary), just a few years after the introduction of the iPod and iTunes. Apple changed popular culture again when the iPhone jump-started an entirely new way of interacting and communicating through ubiquitous access to the Internet using smartphones and the thousands of apps created for their use. Steve Jobs was clearly an entrepreneur. He was also engaged in continuous innovation to identify and create new products and services for unknown or unrealized parts of the market. He was invested in the entrepreneurship process.

Paradoxically, despite the central role entrepreneurs play in markets, early economists focused little attention on entrepreneurship and entrepreneurs. Modern "neoclassical" economics emerged during the industrial revolutions in Europe and the United States. Most economists simply assumed that companies, whether artisan, craft, partnership or corporation, would maximize profits. These profits would provide the incentives that led to innovation. How innovation happened was less important than the fact it did (and taken for granted in market economies). The task of the business owner was to produce as much of a product (or service) as possible at the lowest cost to the consumer so they could compete in the market and maximize profits. The assumption was that market competition would drive business owners and managers to reduce costs and maximize market value. Much of the early contributions to microeconomics—the economics of the individual firm, consumer, and market—revolved around how to determine the most output at the lowest cost. The subdiscipline of managerial economics focused primarily on different techniques for achieving these goals.

The view of the manager as technician (scientific management) evolved as more and more economists explored the frontiers of "the firm" to include entrepreneurial elements of management such as risk taking, discovery, and judgement into more staid conceptions. As Nicolai Foss and Peter G. Klein write in the *Handbook of Entrepreneurship*, "entrepreneurship consists of judgmental decision-making under conditions of uncertainty. Judgement refers primarily to business decision-making when the range of possible future outcomes, let alone the likelihood of individual outcomes, is generally unknown." Entrepreneurship, in this context, is active and can be exercised in very "mundane" situations, not just when decisions imply boldness or high stakes.

This view of entrepreneurship has implications for when a business, or pop music band, might be formed. Band members typically play different roles. The particular combinations of bandmates, and the way their styles converge (or diverge), creates a distinctive sound, allowing them to differentiate themselves from competitors. Few listeners to popular music in the 1960s, for example, would confuse the surf rock sound of the Beach Boys with the hard rock sound of the Who, or the blues-rock grounded Rolling Stones, or the Beatles.

The internal organization and dynamic of the Beatles, however, adds another layer to the understanding of entrepreneurship and the firm. Economists in the tradition of the so-called Austrian School of Economics have probably done the most to explore the nature of a firm's assets and how they contribute to the productivity, efficiency, and innovation inherent in any given business. These economists, including Nobel Prize winner F. A. Hayek, have long recognized that "capital," the physical assets of a corporation, are not unitary or homogeneous. Rather, assets can be deployed in a variety of different ways, depending on the firm (band), or entrepreneur's judgement. Assets are "heterogeneous," comprised of a number of different attributes. A straightforward example might be an automobile. Most people use automobiles for personal mobility, getting from point A to point B efficiently. But automobiles can be used for a variety of different uses depending on the needs or desires of the owner. They can transport freight. They can serve as a home. They can serve as schools. They have been used as pop-up retail shops and restaurants. They can serve as farm equipment. They have even been used to run ski lifts (by taking a rubber tire off and putting a cable on the rim.) The highest and best use of the asset is determined by the entrepreneur, who is organizing her assets to maximize their use in the production process.

In the context of the Beatles, Paul McCartney was not just a songwriter. He was also a guitar player, a pianist, a bass player, a drummer. Sometimes his role was primarily as a collaborator. He served frequently as a producer. He eventually became a more traditional business owner when the multimedia firm Apple Corps was established. As an "asset" that made up the Beatles, he contained a "bundle" of attributes that could be deployed depending how he would create value according to his judgement, or the judgement of the band. The four primary assets that made up the Beatles—Lennon, McCartney, Harrison, and Starr—were not interchangeable parts even though they had defined and visible roles. Disputes also arose over how to deploy the assets. In the swamp blues-inspired song "Oh! Darling" (*Abbey Road*) John Lennon believed his voice had the tone, sound, and style more suitable to the raspy power McCartney wanted to project. Indeed, in the early songs, Lennon was the lead vocal on more traditional rock songs such as "Twist and Shout." Lennon relented because it was, in the end, McCartney's song and he was entitled to record the song as he saw fit.

Traditional views of business, or the "firm," implicitly assume one manager serves in an executive position as president or chief executive officer (CEO) with top-down responsibilities. Leadership is hierarchical. The goal of the manager is to create an organizational structure that ensures the workers below him produce as much as possible with the highest possible quality. Traditional teaching on managerial economics, industrial organization, organizational economics, and even the economics of the industry focuses on this implicitly hierarchical profit-maximizing model.

George Martin's description of the way he initially approached the Beatles is an example of how the traditional mindset is put into action. A producer, he points out, "was basically an organizer" when the Beatles arrived. He would give feedback on the performance, determine which songs would go on the disc, hire session musicians, arrange the logistics of the recording time. This is how Martin looked at the Beatles during their first recording sessions—as discrete elements of a music production company. He tested each one in terms of their role in the group, concluding that "Paul had a sweeter voice, John's had more character, and George generally not so good." More infamously, he encouraged the band to fire Pete Best, their drummer (although others in the band were already thinking about this). When Ringo Starr was hired to replace Best, Martin still retained a more polished session drummer to record with them on their first single, "Love Me Do." The idea was that musicians were largely interchangeable parts although each one had a particular characteristic that could enhance the quality of the overall package if organized the right way. The internal workings and creative process of the Beatles shows this traditional approach is not particularly useful.

John Lennon's role in the start-up of his skiffle bands and the Quarrymen, the direct predecessor of the Beatles, was similar in terms of internal organizational approach. The Quarrymen was formed in 1956 and consisted of Lennon's high school friends. Members would rotate in and out, but it was Lennon who approved new members. McCartney auditioned for Lennon, and joined in 1957. McCartney also deferred to Lennon's judgement and decisions consistently until disagreements began to split the band apart in the late 1960s (after the death of long-time manager and confidant Brian Epstein). Indeed, McCartney pressed Lennon for several months to invite George Harrison to join the band based on his talent despite his relative youth.

Ronald Coase would eventually earn a Nobel Prize in Economics (in 1991) in part for his contribution to explaining why firms exist in a 1937 paper titled "The Nature of the Firm." Essentially, Coase introduced the concept of "transaction costs" to explain why people organize themselves into a company to produce goods and services. Since it's too costly to contract out the production of some services, they are internalized. A senior manager or owner explicitly makes the decision about how to organize a firm to most efficiently produce its product.

In a very general sense this framework can certainly apply to the Beatles as well as other bands. The Beatles were a coherent team, not a collection of session musicians hired to perform specific tasks. Members of the team could contribute to how the product is designed, implemented, and sold on the market. Lennon served as the leader, particularly in the early years, controlling membership in the band, granting access to its valuable privileges (e.g., regular playing time, access to audiences) and providing access to the creative input from the other members. The organizational structure of decision making shifted when Paul McCartney became a more established member as others left the Quarrymen. McCartney's stature was heightened by his relatively superior proficiency as a guitarist and interest in songwriting. McCartney and George Harrison spent hours laboring over new chords, rhythms and playing styles of the artists they would cover on stage. George Harrison benefited from the business ambition and discipline provided by McCartney as well as the musical inspiration of John Lennon. Notably, the four Beatles that ended up defining the band's sound were the product of an evolutionary and organic process of creation, dissolution, and reformation of the band from 1956 when John Lennon formed the Quarrymen until 1962 when Ringo Starr replaced Pete Best as the drummer.

To achieve commercial success, the band needed to coalesce around a stable membership, with significant commitment to the larger organizational entity— the Beatles—before they could launch onto a more prominent stage. This would have been much more difficult if each member of the Beatles was playing in another band, as was common in the amateur world of skiffle, or working as a solo artist. An example of the difficulty surrounding using session musicians—a contracting or outsourcing model—is encapsulated in the experience the band had with Ringo Starr. When Starr left Rory Storm and the Hurricanes for the Beatles, he was already well known to the other members. Starr had watched them play in Hamburg and sat in as drummer on several sessions. When the limits of Pete Best's drumming became apparent, the band dropped him and replaced him with Starr. The fit was so solid, Starr would later recall during their most raucous concerts he would keep the beat by watching the back of John Lennon as he moved to the music. The tightness of the band came from thousands of hours of playing together on stages in Hamburg and in Great Britain. The same quality of musicianship simply could not be replicated by session musicians except in carefully scripted roles.

Transaction costs and the innovation process

But the transaction cost paradigm in economics only goes so far. While the general concept of transaction costs helps understand why the band formed and stayed together, these concepts provide little insight into the innovation process that made the Beatles so influential. A number of bands existed contemporaneously with the Beatles and were commercially successful, but the Beatles' success was unparalleled. Part of the transaction costs paradigm's limitation is that most of its theory is grounded in "static analysis," looking at a specific outcome given an unchanging range of preferences and technologies. This focus on "comparative statics" leads managerial economics and human-resource management to focus narrowly on incentives facing specific leaders and decision makers within certain institutionalized constraints. Thus, Pete Best was fired from the Beatles after pressure from their record label as well as a growing awareness among the other members of the band that his drumming skills were preventing them from producing higher quality music. As George Martin later commented on his reaction to hearing their audition in his memoir, "Frankly, the material didn't impress me, least of all their own songs." The band needed to break through their institutionalized constraints, including changing members, if they wanted to get better and achieve higher levels of success.

Incentives, of course, matter. Organizations also need leaders. Leaders set the direction of the organization, inspire workers to produce, and identify optimal strategies for using resources. Until recently, economics has tended to focus more on the administrative management of businesses rather than their entrepreneurial elements. The classic contributions to theory and organizational behavior were significant and meaningful: The idea that an individual had a stake in their business, and this sense of personal or practical ownership was an important motivator and defined relationships between other members of the firm. More formally, "principal–agent" analysis, where a company owner (the principal) would be tasked with making sure that a service provider (the agent) would perform their assigned tasks at their highest level, became central to the economic understanding of the firm (and later governance more generally). When principals were unable to adequately monitor the performance of agents outside the firm—the costs of monitoring, enforcing, and creating contracts—they would internalize these costs by forming a company. The formation of the Beatles was less focused on "enforcing" contracts, but the inclusion and solidification of the core band members did reduce transaction costs and minimize principal–agent problems. These benefits from consolidation into one organization were critical to the rise of the Beatles but also became a liability when the band was unable to adapt to the creative desires of the individual members. Nevertheless, until recently, most formal economic models have provided little insight into the nature, motivations, and success of entrepreneurs.

Perhaps the frustration of formal modeling is best illustrated by the failure of so-called "behavioral models" to explain why some people become entrepreneurs and others don't. The research is mixed, at best, on whether entrepreneurs have a bias toward optimism, are inclined to take more risks than the general population, overestimate their abilities, underestimate the abilities of their competitors, or generally respond to financial reward. In fact, entrepreneurs tend to earn lower returns on their investments than non-entrepreneurs, according to Thomas Åstebro, Holger Herz, Ramana Nanda, and Roberto A. Weber in a review of the economic and entrepreneurship literature published in the *Journal of Economic Perspectives*. In fact, entrepreneurial motivations appear to be non-monetary (or "nonpecuniary"):

> Taken together, evidence from the field—specifically, the observed compensating differentials and the complementary survey evidence—strongly suggest that nonpecuniary benefits may play an important role in the decision to become and remain an entrepreneur.
>
> *(Åstebro et al. 2014: 664)*

This is certainly consistent with what we know of the Beatles, particularly early in their career.

While the Beatles were ambitious, and very much wanted to be "rich," wealth was hardly a driving force for their creativity and innovation. All the members of the Beatles invested heavily in their bands without significant potential for financial rewards. They were hoping to just get to the point they could sustain themselves financially. Financial sustainability happened four years after the formation of the Quarrymen when their first Hamburg residency was secured, but even then they were living with their parents. In fact, John Lennon could not even imagine himself in a job other than working as an artist, poet, or musician, and he consistently made decisions that worked against full-time regular employment. Ringo Starr worked briefly for British Rail, as a server on a boat, and as an apprentice machinist in a school equipment manufacturer before giving the work up for the more uncertain, less lucrative job as a drummer. Paul McCartney was filling job applications for the Royal Mail when he thought he would need to get a job to support his girlfriend and a family. Their love of music, and their joy in their performances, reflected a personal calling to the industry. The collaborative nature of the Beatles' decision making seen in the later periods of the band, such as Lennon relenting to McCartney on the vocal recording of "Oh! Darling," does not fit well into the traditional model. Fortunately, economists have increasingly recognized the limits of this simplistic top-down model, which is essentially a factory-based approach to labor.

Recently, economics as a discipline has put more emphasis on entrepreneurship and the role innovation plays in firm competitiveness. John Estill and Tom Means, economists at San José State University, for example, surveyed 27 textbooks on the principles of economics and found most at least mentioned entrepreneurship. More than half listed entrepreneurship as a separate factor of production independent of labor, capital, and land. But entrepreneurship is more than just a variable in a formula or production function, and the internal workings of the Beatles show why. The entrepreneur is not simply a manager allocating resources to their most profitable uses.

A new vision for entrepreneurship

Economist Israel Kirzner laid out these principles and insights in *Competition and Entrepreneurship* and other writings during the 1970s and 1980s. Entrepreneurs are not merely people who own businesses or, for that matter, maximize profits. Entrepreneurs are looking for new opportunities that the market has left unexploited. The "pure entrepreneur," Kirzner writes, is "a decision-maker whose *entire* role arises out of his alertness to hitherto unnoticed opportunities." Entrepreneurs use articulated information as well as tacit information and intuition to identify new niches, new products, and new services the customers are willing to pay for. The entrepreneur is a disruptor, someone who pushes beyond existing products and services provided. Economist Randall G. Holcombe takes this concept a step even further in *Entrepreneurship and Economic Progress*: Entrepreneurs do more than recognize new opportunities, they exploit them. Both agree that entrepreneurship "means implementing something new," not simply maximizing the use of conventional inputs. Entrepreneurship is a creative process as well as a commercial one. Management icon Peter Drucker takes this a step further in his influential book *Innovation and Entrepreneurship*, claiming "Successful entrepreneurs, whatever their motivation ... try to create value and to make a contribution."

The difference between management and entrepreneurship is important, Holcombe observes. The "institutional structure that leads to effective management is different from the institutions that lead entrepreneurial activity," he writes. "For a firm to survive in the long run, good management is helpful but successful entrepreneurship is essential." The entrepreneur must continually update, improve, and invent new products to be successful and maintain its place in the competitive marketplace.

How do these abstract ideas work in practice? The innovation process embedded in the Beatles' songwriting and performances provide an intriguing window for seeing them in the real world. "Innovation is the specific tool of entrepreneurs," notes Drucker, "the means by which they exploit change as an opportunity for a different business or a different service." The Beatles show how this works in practice.

On the surface, the Beatles had a conventional division of labor—John Lennon on rhythm guitar, Paul McCartney on bass guitar, George Harrison on lead guitar, and Ringo Starr on drums. They performed these instruments masterfully in their performances. In practice, however, the division of labor was not so distinct. With the possible exception of Ringo Starr, the other three bandmates experimented widely with other instruments as well as sounds. Lennon would play lead guitar as well as keyboards. Harrison became well known for his experimentation with

Indian music in popular songs. McCartney may have been the most versatile, playing keyboards, guitar, bass guitar, and drums at various times. When Martin infused orchestral arrangements, their music-making versatility expanded dramatically and continuously over the course of their career as the Beatles.

They also innovated constantly throughout their career challenging the shibboleths of the times. In the 1950s and 1960s, rock music was considered the antithesis of classical music. Yet Lennon's "Because" was inspired by Beethoven's "Moonlight Sonata," which included double overdubbing of triple harmonies. Musicologist Steve Turner notes "There was a touch of irony in the idea of a Beatle borrowing from Beethoven because there was a common perception at the time that rock and roll was antithetical to classical music and that no one could genuinely appreciate both." Similarly, the guitar work in McCartney's classic "Blackbird" was inspired by Bach. Their commitment to innovation was also authentic. David Mason, for example, the session musician playing trumpet on "Penny Lane," was impressed that Lennon, Harrison, and Starr were also in the recording studio even though it was McCartney (arranged by George Martin) who scripted the element into the song. They retained a keen interest in all aspects of song production, and this was apparent to those who spent time in the recording studio.

The band (and Martin) was also willing to tap into the best talent possible. Mason was recognized as a top-quality musician in London at the time the Beatles were engaged in the *Sgt. Pepper* recording sessions in 1966 and 1967 although his specialty was classical music. During the mid-1960s, former music producer Peter Asher recalls the standard "scale" for a session musician was about £9 (about US$22) per session at the exchange rate at the time. After accounting for inflation, this rate translates into about US$180 per session for about an hour's worth of work.

Some musicians, such as Mason, were paid more. According to Asher, Mason was paid the "recital fee" of £56 (equivalent to about $1,200 today), for his classic piccolo trumpet work on "Penny Lane." Mason, however, recalls being paid a flat fee of US$45 (about US$350 in current dollars). Wikipedia cites Mason's session fee as equivalent to about £26 (US$65 at the time, or a little over US$500 in current dollars). The price did not scare the Beatles or George Martin away: Mason played on subsequent recordings, including "A Day in the Life," "All You Need is Love," "Magical Mystery Tour." and "It's All Too Much."

Many people have understandably attributed the Beatles success to the songwriting talents of John Lennon and Paul McCartney. But their partnership was not a typical one. They were not a "duo," observes Todd Lowry, an industry attorney and musician who arranged *The Complete Beatles* for the music publisher Hal Leonard, LLC. Lowry identified true collaboration between the two on just 18 recorded Beatles songs. Lennon wrote 72 songs largely on his own while McCartney wrote 70, an almost even split by Lowry's count. Lennon and McCartney were a far cry from other true writing partners such as the Rolling Stones' Mick Jagger and Keith Richards.

Most often, Lennon or McCartney would have their songs mostly written before they brought them to each other (or the band), and each would help the other "finish it off." Similarly, George Harrison's songs were largely complete in their essentials before the rest of the band, mostly Lennon and McCartney, would tweak the words and music, or George Martin arrange an orchestral composition. Particularly in the later years, songs went through dozens of takes as they experimented with different styles and approaches. "Revolution," for example, was initially recorded as a slower, bluesy song before taking on its final hard rock version. Thus, for the Beatles, songwriting was a creative collaboration rather than a strict division of labor or well-defined partnership.

The Beatles also established their culture of collaboration and innovation early on. As their band began to gain a following, they found themselves climbing the rungs of the play bill toward the lead position. McCartney now recalls how they would listen to the early acts, and realize they were playing the same songs in their sets. In order to stay at the top of the play bill, and keep their audience, they had to start playing different songs. Lennon, McCartney, and Harrison began mining the B-sides of popular songs coming from the US and charting in Britain. This practice helped define their fresh sound and on-stage drive that ignited audiences. The songwriting came out of necessity if they wanted to stay competitive. As McCartney told David Frost in 2012:

> So we had to start looking for B-sides and unusual tracks, and then started to think we might try writing some. So, none of this kind of "the great muse came upon us"—the Lennon/McCartney muse—there was none of that. It was just we needed to so they couldn't get at our songs.

Another critical part of their process that became infused in the band's culture was the need to innovate. McCartney and Lennon were the gatekeepers for the recorded songs released on records. This created a problem for the band in the years immediately leading to the break-up, but their relentless pursuit of new sounds and song structure created a culture of experimentation and a willingness to be open to and exploit new opportunities in the pop music market. Anything could "go" as long as it sounded good and interesting. They would write and approve songs that would change tempo, change keys, and include unconventional song structures. Many of these innovations became signature elements of pop music and the Beatles distinctive sound.

These innovations also reflected a bit of serendipity. During the recording of "I Feel Fine," Lennon leaned his guitar against an amplifier, generating feedback. Combined with a note plucked from McCartney's bass guitar, the song became the first known use of feedback on a recorded song and helped, along with its catchy guitar riffs, make it a classic. The song topped the US and UK charts in 1964 and 1965.

An example of a more deliberative approach to innovation is the opening chord on the song "A Hard Day's Night." The song itself is deceptively simple. Lennon wrote the song in one night, and McCartney helped polish it off the next morning. The band recorded nine takes and were done within three hours. One element the band and George Martin were looking for was a strong, distinctive opening since the song would be the first song on the soundtrack and heard in the film *A Hard Day's Night*. The instruments used by the musicians contributed to the effect, most notably a 12-string electric guitar played by George Harrison combined with Paul McCartney on the bass guitar, John Lennon on an acoustic six-string guitar, George Martin on the piano, and Ringo Starr on drums.

Thus, the Beatles were open to new opportunities to create music in ways that engaged their listeners, pushing the envelope on popular music. "Strawberry Fields Forever" was a path-breaking song recorded in November and December 1966 that infused studio, sound, and song structure elements unheard of before this time. After spending dozens of hours recording different versions of the song—longer than any other song Lennon recorded, according to EMI sound engineer Geoff Emerick—Lennon announced he liked the beginning of another version. "So, what I'd like our young Geoffrey here to do is to join the two bits together," Emerick recalls in his memoir *Here, There and Everywhere*. The only problem, Martin reminded him, was that the two versions (take 7 and take 26) were recorded in different keys and at different speeds. With some experimentation, Emerick says, "I discovered that by speeding up the playback on the first take and slowing down the playback on the second, I could get them to match both pitch and tempo." The result was, in Emerick's words, a "landmark recording." Backwards recording was also incorporated into this song, although the technique had been used before (e.g., "Rain" on *Revolver*). This time, however, Beatles fans interpreted the backwards recording as saying "Paul is dead," launching a worldwide panic and urban legend. But "Strawberry Fields" had other less magical innovations as well, including an orchestral fusion ending that faded out and then faded back in what music theorist Walter Everett has called a "free-form coda." The song was a long way from their 90 minute recording sessions per song on the first album. "Strawberry Fields Forever" logged 45 hours in the studio and 26 takes over five weeks.

"Strawberry Fields," however, is just one example of many types of innovations. George Harrison's gradual introduction of Indian instruments added unusual and unexpected textures to their songs as early as *Rubber Soul* (released in 1965). "Norwegian Wood" is the first known use of a sitar on a pop music record. Harrison also used Indian musician Anil Baghwat to play the sitar and tabla on "Love You Too" (1966). A variety of experimental recording techniques were used to record "Tomorrow Never Knows," a dramatic aesthetic break from early rock and foreshadowing their psychedelic phase of experimentation that would grip the band during the *Sgt. Pepper* recording sessions. This experimentation might appear to be ad hoc, but the process was institutionalized into a song-writing process that was central to the evolution of the Beatles from the very beginning.

Sustained innovation

The sustained evolution of the Beatles sound is a good example of the distinction between invention and innovation, a difference popularized through the work of economist Joseph Schumpeter in his book *The Theory of Economic Development* in the 1930s. Innovation is a process, an ongoing series of activities that leads to new ways of doing things or producing goods and services. Invention, in contrast, is the creation of specific products and outputs. One of the inventions exploited in the studio, for example, was tape looping. Another was the unconventional use of speakers to change the sound of a guitar or voice (such as a "tunnel effect" used for John Lennon's voice in "Tomorrow Never Knows"). These innovations were created within a process that encouraged the discovery and acting on new ways a creating and experiencing music. The consistent use or creation of inventions to change a product is innovation.

What the Beatles were doing from the very beginning was creating a process of sustained invention. First, the innovation happened on stage as they interpreted their music with a high level of energy and sassiness that differentiated themselves from their contemporaries as well as using three-part harmonies among the three front men. But they continued to differentiate themselves. Since the bands in the 1950s were drawing from the same playlists (usually American rock and roll, jazz, R&B, or country), they looked for cover songs that were different from the standards. They differentiated themselves again when they started writing and playing their own songs. As McCartney has said numerous times in interviews, the only requirement was that whatever song was being proposed was different from anything they had done before or was already out on the market. This ingrained focus on creating songs that were new, or had a new element, created a set of values and work rules that sustained innovation.

Management expert Peter Drucker writes in his book *Innovation and Entrepreneurship*, "*Systemic innovation therefore consists in the purposeful and organized search for changes, and in the systematic analysis of the opportunities such changes might offer for economic and social innovation*" (Drucker 2015: 35; emphasis in original). This was what John Lennon and Paul McCartney were instilling in the creative DNA of the Beatles as far back as 1957. Moreover, they did not just establish the creative values of the Beatles. They also adopted rules and protocols for ensuring innovation was always at the center of their creative enterprise. They were, in effect, managing innovation. As entrepreneurship expert Joseph Maciariello notes in the foreword to the Routledge Classics edition of Drucker's work (Drucker 2015: xii): "The work of the entrepreneur is to innovate and to successfully manage innovation."

How successful were the Beatles in innovating? The more than 200 songs recorded in the studio and released as singles on albums contributed to more than 60 music genres and subgenres. Beatles songs have been tagged with more than 300 different genres. Some of these songs are so innovative they charted new territory. Their innovation is illustrated in the increasing diversity of the

Beatles catalogue of recorded music over time. As they launched their career, the Beatles music was firmly ensconced in their roots in rock and roll, including skiffle, Merseybeat, and R&B (Figure 3.2). As they entered the mid-1960s, their music diversified into the relatively lighter versions of folk and country music. As they progressed through the 1960s, their music was increasingly characterized by experimental forms, including orchestral arrangements in Baroque (e.g., "Eleanor Rigby," "Hey Jude") and then the groundbreaking psychedelic sounds of "Strawberry Fields Forever" and "Lucy in the Sky With Diamonds" that led directly to *Sgt. Pepper Lonely Hearts Club Band* and *The Beatles* (aka the *White Album*).

Entrepreneurship, then, is more than just making a current input more technically efficient—improving George Harrison's guitar skills, making John Lennon more versatile on his instrument, or tweaking a line of a lyric. An entrepreneur is not simply "doing the same things better," as Holcombe observes. "It means doing different things that create more value than the previous way of doing things." Thus, the benefit of innovation is more than simply making changes on the margin. Rather, the outcome is creating new value that has broad-based impacts. To put this in a broader context, the next chapter takes a deeper dive into what was widely considered the most experimental (and commercially successful) album of their career: *Sgt. Pepper's Lonely Hearts Club Band*.

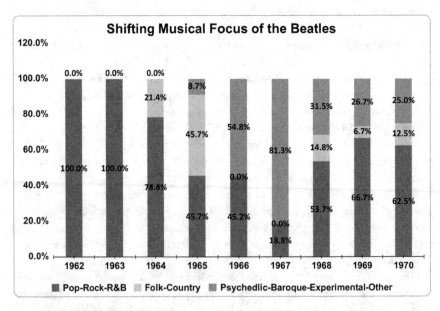

FIGURE 3.2 Shifting musical focus of the Beatles
Source: Created by the author from Wikipedia, "List of Songs Recorded by the Beatles," last accessed by author June 25, 2019

References

Åstebro, Thomas, Holger Herz, Ramana Nanda, and Roberto A. Weber. 2014. "Seeking the Roots of Entrepreneurship: Insights from Behavioral Economics," *Journal of Economic Perspectives*, 28(3), 49–70.

Coase, Ronald. 1937. "The Nature of the Firm," *Economica*, 4(16), 386–405.

Drucker, Peter. 2015. *Innovation and Entrepreneurship*. London: Routledge Classics.

Dweck, Carol S. 2007. *Mindset: The New Psychology of Success*. New York: Ballantine Books.

Elmer, Vickie. 2016. "Failure: What Can Businesses Learn When Things Go Wrong?," *SAGE Business Researcher*, January 4, reprinted in *Issues in Entrepreneurship & Small Business Management*. Thousand Oaks, CA: Sage Publications, pp. 277–300.

Emerick, Geoff and Howard Massey. 2006. *Here, There and Everywhere: My Life Recording the Music of the Beatles*. New York: Gotham Books.

Estill, John and Tom Means. 2019. "How Do Principles Textbooks Treat the Return to Entrepreneurship? The Missing Factor," *The Journal of Private Enterprise*, 34(3), 35–42.

Flans, Robyn, n.d. "Ringo Starr." Retrieved from www.pas.org/about/hall-of-fame/ringo-starr, last accessed September 3, 2019.

Foss, Nicolai and Peter G. Klein. 2005. "Entrepreneurship and the Economic Theory of the Firm: Any Gains From Trade?". In R. Agarwal, S. A. Alverez, and O. Sorenson, eds, *Handbook of Entrepreneurship: Disciplinary Perspectives*. Norwell, MA: Kluwer.

Holcombe, Randall G. 2007. *Entrepreneurship and Economic Progress*. London: Routledge.

Kirzner, Israel. 1973. *Competition and Entrepreneurship*. Chicago, IL: University of Chicago Press.

Martin, George. 1994. *All You Need Is Ears: The Inside Personal Story of the Genius Who Created the Beatles*. New York: St. Martin's Griffin.

Norman, Philip. 2003. *Shout: The Beatles in Their Generation*, revised edition. New York: Fireside Books.

Schumpeter, Joseph S. 1934. *The Theory of Economic Development*. Cambridge, MA: Harvard University.

Turner, Steve. 2009. *The Beatles: A Hard Day's Write—The Stories Behind Every Song*. New York: MJF Books.

4

HOW PRIVATE MARKETS ENABLED SGT. PEPPER'S BAND TO PLAY

Economic concepts: Economic growth, consumer markets, subjective value, labor markets, income growth, disposable income, market competition

By 1966, the Beatles had emerged as the world's top-grossing musical act. Almost all of this money was generated from albums which were recorded to support their live performances. Their decision to stop touring after their last stage performance (at San Francisco's Candlestick Park in August) was, by industry standards and convention, a potentially cataclysmic event. But, as history shows, the Beatles were anything but over. Indeed, in retrospect, they weren't even close to the summit of their influence over culture and popular music. How could this be?

The seeds of their revolutionary impact were already sown when they decided to stop touring. While their fame and fortunes to this point were built on the foundations of American 1950s rock and roll, rhythm and blues, and country music, the Beatles had already provided fans with a glimpse of their future. George Martin, their producer at EMI/Parlophone could see it, too. Geoff Emerick and other engineers working in the sound studios witnessed it unfold. But the Beatles' evolution as artists, and their influence, were hardly forgone conclusions. The previous chapter discussed the Beatles innovation culture which allowed them to continue to create and add value to their music. This chapter dives deep into the institutional economic forces that allowed them to leverage that creative force to influence the futures of generations and the music they listen to. And it all couldn't have happened without private markets or entrepreneurial capitalism.

Economists use the term "capitalism" in a very specific context. The first known use of the word emerged in 1850 and was coined by French socialist

Louis Blanc. The term became much more broadly used when Karl Marx authored his three-volume treatise *Das Kapital*, or *Capital* (1867, 1885, and 1894). By this time, the economic system of England had over 100 years of transformative experience with the rise of an industrial economy that pulled apart the fabric of the feudal system at its agrarian roots. Individuals were given the freedom to build businesses to meet consumer needs. They used technology and factories to increase output and drive down costs to give a growing middle and working classes access to consumer goods at levels unprecedented in human history. The private corporation, free to produce goods for mass consumption, was crucial to this increase in productivity and income.

Marx, building on theories developed by Adam Smith in *The Wealth of Nations* (1776) and a long tradition in Western philosophical thought, explained the rise of wealth among the business, or "industrial" class, as the exploitation of labor. Marx believed that economic value was derived solely from labor. Since businessmen (and women) did not physically produce the products and services they sold, they were capturing the value of the labor in the form of "capital"—the machinery, equipment, factory, and land they owned to the exclusion of workers.

Marx believed that the labor used to produce goods and services could be measured objectively, hence this theory is also called the "objective" theory of value. The prices of goods and services paid by customers were the "exchange value." The capitalist's profits were the difference between the labor value and the exchange value. In this system, the capitalists become richer by reducing the amount of the exchange value going to labor and maximizing the exchange value going to capital—owners of the means of production. Hence, in a straightforward manner, capitalists "exploit" labor to maximize their personal wealth. Marx's analysis implied that at some point the amount going to labor would be so low that the workers (proletariat) would experience mass unemployment, recognize the injustice of the capitalist system, and rise up against the capitalists (bourgeoisie) in a worker-led revolution.

The Smith–Marx view of wealth creation seems quite logical and rational when viewed from the perspective of art. Few people, for example, would argue that "art" is produced by anything other than the creator of that art. The extent middle men or owners of capital earned profits from the art, and revenues above and beyond what was necessary to directly purchase equipment (e.g., recording equipment, vinyl pressing machines, trucks to transport records), would be considered exploitive.

Fortunately, the Beatles did not hold this view of value creation. Indeed, the success of the Beatles, both culturally and economically, is an illustration of the theoretical and practical limitations of an objective labor theory of value.

Art and economic value

The labor theory has been replaced in contemporary "neoclassical" economics by what is called "subjective value." Neoclassical economists—who can be distinguished from institutional, Keynesian, neo-Keynesian, behavioral, or other schools of eco-nomics—see value as the product of consumer choice and preferences determined in a price-driven market system. Market prices reflect what consumers are willing to pay for a good or service. Producers will determine whether they will provide a good or service based on whether they can employ the inputs—labor, land, machinery, raw materials, creative talent, etc.—at a price sufficient to cover their costs (which includes the financial returns entrepreneurs need to compensate them for the risks and effort needed to secure financing, purchase the goods, market the goods, and establish distribution systems of various sorts).

In practice, even though they were not trained as economists or in economics, the Beatles' working knowledge of the economy was rooted in this market-based, consumer-driven theory of value. As individuals, each of the Beatles has talked about how they really wanted to become wealthy as musicians or songwriters. While becoming rich was not the driving force of their vocational choice, it was one of their objectives. More importantly, the personal wealth they accumulated as artists was seen as a validation of their work. The more people listened to their music, the more concert tickets they sold, the more records their fans bought, the more the value of their work could be monetized through the economy. In this sense, they recognized, implicitly, that market value is a social construct, not a personal one. The could toil in their rooms or homes writing and playing songs, but unless listeners validated their work in the market, the value would always be lower—regardless of how much effort they put into writing, recording, and play-ing their songs.

This way of looking at value—as consumer driven and created—gave the Beatles an important perspective that would serve them well, as artists and influencers on the broader cultural (and political) landscape. The Beatles' artistic origins are telling in this respect. Unlike many well-known twenty-first-century bands, the Beatles started strictly as a cover band. They played popular songs that had already been validated in the marketplace. Consumers—teenagers—validated this value by buying records from the original artists and then packing clubs and theaters to hear bands such as the Beatles, the Dave Clark Five, Rory Storm and the Hurricanes, and hundreds of others perform. This was the foundation of the skiffle craze in England that led to the formation of the Quarrymen by John Lennon and his schoolmates. The bands that successfully found an audience, and were validated by attracting larger audiences, were successful, eventually securing record deals and concert tours at the national and international levels.

This subjective approach to value also served the Beatles in other capacities. They realized as their fame grew, and their name climbed closer to the top of play bills, that they had to create new material to compete. They had to add value. They had to contribute to the inventory of pop music in ways that satisfied the wants and preferences of their audiences. Once they had mined the useful material from existing artists, they started writing their own.

Perhaps no project better illustrates the power of market validation for a product produced by the Beatles than the steps leading up to the production and commercial success of the album *Sgt. Pepper's Lonely Hearts Club Band*. The album ranks among the most important pop music albums of the twentieth century. Working with Parlophone executive George Martin and sound engineer Geoff Emerick, the Beatles engaged break-through uses of the studio, including extensive and pioneering techniques such as automatic double-tracking, signal limiting, dynamic range compression, reverberation, direct injection of instruments into the recording console, changing the speed and tempo of songs, close-miking of drums and other innovations which created innovative and progressive sounds. More importantly, the album was a massive commercial success, an unusual blend of cutting-edge artistry and monetization through the marketplace.

What enabled the Beatles to produce this particular album with this scale and impact? Traditional explanations have focused on the artistry—the album was part of the Beatles creative process and evolution—the role of their entrepreneurial producer and engineers (George Martin, Geoff Emerick, etc.), and their platform as the biggest musical act in the world. These are pieces of the puzzle, but fall short on their own. Pop music, after all, is a commercial enterprise. Any explanation without understanding market and business dynamics can't put the pieces together in a coherent puzzle. Economic analysis provides the insight necessary to create a more holistic explanation for their success and their sustained influence fifty years later.

The Beatles achieved a historic milestone in 1964 when they became the first British band to top the American music charts, with "I Want to Hold Your Hand." The Beatles had broken into the charts in early 1964 with "Please Please Me," and they dominated the charts by the end of 1964 and throughout 1965. Beatles songs held the top four spots at the end of the year rankings on Billboard's Hot 100 list, and eight songs overall making the top 100. The band played several American tours as movies such as *A Hard Day's Night* and *Help!* were released, and singles off the albums *Rubber Soul* and *Revolver* began to chart.

Of particular note is their 1966 tour which took them around the USA and then on to Japan and Philippines. The Asian tour was problematic because of several controversies over cultural conflict in Japan and political conflict surrounding the authoritarian Marcos regime in Manila. The Beatles had to be rushed to their plane to leave the Philippines or risk physical violence based on a perceived snub of the dictator. Also, during this tour, John Lennon made the controversial statement that The Beatles were "more popular than Jesus," setting off protests and album burnings in the American South and other socially conservative circles.

Concerns for their personal safety, combined with the eroding quality of their live music venues (the crowds were so loud Ringo Starr couldn't hear the music) led to a formal decision to stop touring after their performance at San Francisco's Candlestick Park (Giants Stadium) in 1966. This choice should have been the economic death knell for a pop music group. Instead, it unleashed an unprecedented spurt of creativity and innovation. More importantly, their creativity and commitment to innovation was fully monetized in the consumer market. How? And why the Beatles?

Economic and social context

As discussed in Chapter 1, World War II devastated European and Asian economies. These economies were already weak from the trials of the Great Depression during the 1930s. Prior to the war, western Europe and Japan ranked among the world's most prosperous industrial economies. Five years of "total" warfare left these economies in shambles, with major industrial cities effectively leveled from carpet bombing. Japan's economy suffered from two atomic bombs that devastated the key industrial cities of Hiroshima and Nagasaki, while critical German manufacturing centers such as Dusseldorf, Hamburg, and Dresden experienced near annihilation. Except for the United States and Canada, each economy needed to rebuild.

After 1960, however, these major world economies began to grow dramatically (see Figure 4.1). The US economy expanded by 75 percent over the decade, from about $3,000 per capita to $5,247 per capita by 1970 (in current dollars), according to the World Bank's World Development Indicators. The UK's economy grew by 70 percent during the same period while Japan's economy more than tripled in output. Indeed, the group of nations that made up the Organisation for Economic Co-operation and Development (OECD) experienced rapid growth in the 1950s and 1960s as they rebuilt their economies. "In the 1950s and 1960s many OECD countries grew rapidly towards the much higher US income levels," economists wrote in *OECD World Economic Outlook 67*, "partly through imported US technologies and knowledge but also, in some cases, as a result of post-war reconstruction." This growth fueled a massive expansion of household income. For the

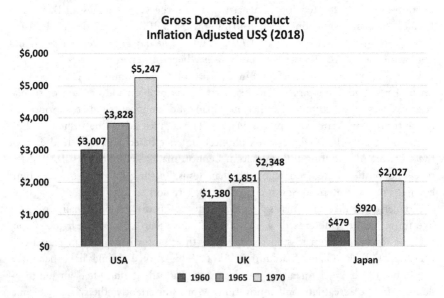

FIGURE 4.1 Growth in Gross Domestic Product for USA, UK, and Japan, 1960 to 1970
Source: World Development Indicators, World Bank, Washington, DC

first time since before the Great Depression, households were achieving levels of wealth that allowed them to expand their consumption beyond necessities such as housing, food, and transportation. More importantly for the Beatles and popular music, this wealth enabled an increase in fertility and the dramatic expansion of a youth consumer base.

The US population may again represent the clearest example of how these demographic trends shifted and what it meant for pop music's consumer base. As would be expected, low fertility during the Great Depression and World War II resulted in stagnant growth in the teenage cohorts. After 1950, how-ever, as the post-War baby boom took hold, pre-teen and teenage cohorts increased dramatically. These demographic groups represented 33 million people in 1950, and increased to 40 million in 1960. By 1970, the core market had expanded to 46 million. More importantly, the growth of these demo-graphic groups reinforced each other. As the pre- and young-teen market matured into the teen market, and then evolved into young adults, the size of the overall market grew exponentially.

More teenagers were entering the workforce and earning their own income during this period as well. The employable teenage population (16 to 19 years old) increased from 8.3 million in 1955 to 12.9 million in 1965 to 15.7 million in 1973. The number of teenagers employed increased from 3.6 million in 1955 to 7.2 million in 1973. Teenage male labor force participation rates hovered near 60 percent in 1955 and 1973 after dipping to just 50 percent in 1965 according to the US Department of Labor. Female participation rates increased from 39.7 percent in 1955 to 47.8 percent in 1973 (after dipping to 38 percent in 1965). Thus, teenagers were becoming more numerous and had access to more discre-tionary income.

Not surprisingly, the growth trends favored the dramatic expansion of products and services geared toward the youth market. The Beatles were riding this wave which didn't crest until the 1990s. To some extent, the Beatles were benefiting from serendipity. They were arriving on the scene at the right time.

The growth of this primary market for popular music, however, was not necessarily a sufficient condition to bring the Beatles to prominence in pop music, let alone dominance. The people making up this part of popular demography had to become consumers in the market by monetizing the value of their preferences through purchases of products that appealed to them. These funds would either come from willing parents or from their own wages. In addition, the Beatles had competition from a wide range of alternatives. Motown was producing steady streams of talented artists who were charting in the US and UK. Rock and roll music, the source of their inspiration, was growing in these markets as well. The Beatles benefitted from being ahead of the curve, but only slightly.

Thus, three fundamental demographic and economic trends combined to create a solid foundation for the growth of youth-oriented popular culture: post-World War II economic recovery, rising numbers of teenagers and young adults, and increasing discretionary income among those most likely to buy their records.

In more explicit economic terms, wealth creation was central to establishing the economic base necessary to support discretionary activities such as entertainment. Some of this wealth was monetized by the core demographic—teenagers and young adults—through wages. This created a substantially growing market that benefited the Beatles (and other popular artists). By the time the Beatles stopped touring, each member of the band was independently wealthy. They were touring for the joy of live performances, not because they needed more money.

Enriching the individual Beatles was a necessary but not sufficient condition for the creation of *Sgt. Pepper's Lonely Hearts Club Band*. The Beatles had to channel that wealth into their musical artistry. This was accomplished through their entrepreneurial "growth mindset" that had emerged as a hallmark of the band's culture and the collaboration between John Lennon and Paul McCartney. This enabled the band to experiment and EMI to give the band an effective "blank check" to use their studios and best talent (producer George Martin, engineer Geoff Emerick, among others). Not all bands had similar cultures or aspirations (although Brian Wilson of the Beach Boys is a notable exception). Their personal and corporate wealth was critical leverage, in part because their contract with EMI required them to use in-house studios. As Geoff Emerick recalls in *Here, There and Everywhere*:

> One major difference between *Revolver* and *Pepper* was that there was an absolute drop-dead date by which *Revolver* had to be completed, because a tour was about to begin. But with *Pepper*, the group could literally take as long as they liked, so they worked on it until they were completely satisfied; there were no other obligations to fulfill. It's possible that, behind the scenes, EMI was lobbying the group to finish it, but by this time they were so huge they were immune to any pressure. The record company simply had to wait until the Beatles themselves were ready to deliver the album.

This history suggests that creating the *Sgt. Pepper's Lonely Hearts Club* album challenges conventional artistic and the traditional economic viewpoints of the firm and their ability to explain innovation in the firm. The rest of this chapter dives deeper into this process.

Creative context

An underappreciated element of the Beatles' creative process is the "growth mindset" discussed in Chapter 3. Their approach to music emphasized creating new experiences for their audiences. Live performances always have an element of spontaneity and interpretation, a unique mix of familiarity (structure) for the audience and improvisation (creativity) from the artists. Very little evidence suggests that the Beatles wanted to stop touring. Not only were the tours a way to monetize their value of their art, performance allowed them to stay in touch with their fans (consumers). The decision to end touring was directly connected to their inability to continue that part of their business as a creative enterprise.

Another element was a growing concern for their personal safety. Their last tour was the one during which John Lennon's off-hand comments about the Beatles being more popular than Jesus were published. The comments unleashed a back-lash that included Beatles record burnings and death threats. At the same time, the crowds at their concerts were becoming increasingly unruly, prompting promoters to hire security to keep them safe. The crazy fans shown running after them in the movie *A Hard Day's Night* became all too real as their personal lives became more and more proscribed. While large concert audio technology was in its infancy, separating the band from their fans became increasingly important as a matter of personal safety. The concert venues no longer provided an effective means for artistic expression despite the vast quantities of money they generated for the pro-moters, their record label, and their own personal bank accounts.

For artists, or "creators," the live shows served little purpose despite their love for performance. More importantly, the Beatles had an alternative: They could go into the studio and record. Their commercial value had proven themselves in the market, and the variety of acts in the pop music world had expanded dra-matically. Bands such as the Yardbirds were experimenting with harmonies in popular and unconventional ways. So-called "psychedelic" music included con-temporaneous acts such as the Byrds, the Beach Boys, and even Bob Dylan, all of whom were were making inroads into the pop music scene before the Beatles jumped in 1966. Some of their predecessors, most notably Brian Wilson (the Beach Boys), were spending more time in the studio as they expanded their craft and created new sounds.

As a practical matter, the recording studio was becoming an important place for creative growth and expression. The band increasingly used the studio as a place to write and create songs, not just refine and record them. The *Rubber Soul* recordings allowed the band to explore new approaches to their music. Some of these new sounds were strikingly retrospective. Stylistically, "Yesterday" (off the *Help!* album) released in 1965, harkened back to the softer, cabaret songs they band had played on their early tours of northern England and in Liverpool. But the recording repre-sented a major creative break from the earlier recordings. As George Martin recalls:

> On "Yesterday" the added ingredient was not more nor less than a string quartet; and that, in the pop world of those days, was quite a step to take. It was with "Yesterday" that we started breaking out of the phase of using just four instruments and went into something more experimental …

"Norwegian Wood" (*Rubber Soul*) is a very conventional (if well-crafted) song in many respects—guitar chord progressions, lyrics about a one-night stand—but introduced the Indian sitar for the first time in pop music. Today, George Harrison's sitar is recognized as one of the signature elements of the song. *Rubber Soul*, however, still had a song list—"Drive My Car," "Nowhere Man," "Girl," "I'm Looking Through You," among others—that was suitable for playing in live venues.

Revolver is often considered by music critics and fans as a more creative and signature departure for the Beatles. The songs represent significant changes in song composition and arrangement as producers and engineers innovated with amplifiers, backward and multiple tape looping, and pushing the limits of the technology in the recording studio. Some of the songs rank among the most experimental in the Beatles canon, including "Tomorrow Never Knows." Many have argued that *Revolver* also represents a major step forward in the band's maturity as song writers. "Here, There and Everywhere" ranks as Paul McCartney's favorite song written as a Beatle because of its structure and lyric. Many of these songs could not have been recreated on stage if the group had continued touring because the technology did not exist to reproduce the sounds live or as playback during their concerts.

The *Sgt. Pepper* sessions represented an even more dramatic departure from their previous recordings. During their first sessions with Parlophone, the Beatles recorded each song in ninety-minute sessions. Their live playing was so tight, and the songs sufficiently straightforward, they could record a song in one or two takes. Their first album of 14 songs (*Please Please Me*) was recorded in just 13 hours, essentially recreating their live performances for each song. They even recorded a fifteenth song ("Hold Me Tight") that was not released with the album. In fact, their contract with EMI had them produce two albums a year. The songs they were performing, combined with their mastery of playing, allowed them to fit this production schedule even as they were recording and producing their own, original material.

Giving up touring had the effect of eliminating two substantial constraints that had delayed their next step in creativity as artists. First, without touring, they had a lot of time on their hands. Tours were grueling efforts, and the band often needed time off to recharge emotionally and creatively. Notably, the Beatles did not return to the recording studio until three months after their final concert in San Francisco.

The second benefit was their ability to spend—or more properly invest—the wealth they had accumulated. While they spent their money on material goods, they also used their human capital in new ways. Rather than earning revenue by touring, they invested their time in the studio, collaborating with each other as well as engineers, George Martin, and other artists to create new material. Unlike previous times, where breaks in playing were considered "free time" they could use in the studio to record another album, the Beatles used this time to create and find inspiration. The Beach Boys, for example, had released *Pet Sounds* by the time the Beatles ended their worldwide tour, and McCartney has acknowledged Brian Wilson's creativity in inspiring part of *Sgt. Pepper's Lonely Hearts Club Band*.

The scale of the band's willingness to push the envelope, and potentially create substantial anxiety among EMI executives, is difficult to underestimate. When the Beatles went into EMI's facilities for their first album, *Please Please Me*, the fifteen songs were recorded (just eight written by Lennon and McCartney), mixed, and edited into their final release-ready form with just 24 hours of studio time. The Beatles would ultimately spend 400 hours in the studios during the *Sgt. Pepper* sessions by April of 1967. EMI and George Martin invested 700 hours in total producing the album by the time it was released the following July. The cost to EMI was sixty times the amount the company had invested in previous albums and acts.

In retrospect, the investment was well worth it—the album has sold more than 37 million copies since its release. But the investment in time and resources was unprecedented. EMI was taking on a substantial investment risk. The fact the executives put so little pressure on the Beatles (and George Martin) is testimony to the value the band had created in the popular music market. The investment was high risk, but they also knew it was potentially very high reward commercially.

Notably, EMI's view was strikingly different from the view of the Beatles—the creators. Given the innovation culture established by the band, and their independent wealth, the commercial and the artistic risks were relatively small compared to other bands or artists. As artists, even for a band whose members were as commercially minded as the Beatles, their ability to create the music they believed was valuable was already assured. Lennon and McCartney, with the implicit consent of Harrison and Starr, allowed only the best quality music to rise to the surface. Moreover, their views on the artistic merit of their music was, as a practical matter, now largely divorced from the need to generate income. While the Beatles still viewed commercial success as a validating consequence of their art, they were even less constrained to produce music that served their existing market. They could take the gamble that most of their fans would follow them into their experimental and new genres. Their gamble paid off.

Wikipedia entries for the music genres for the 1950s, 1960s, 1970s, and 1980s provide some interesting insight into how pop music expanded during the Beatles era. Again, the open source nature of the platform is what makes the entries interesting. The specific data are not curated for style or interpretation. The entries are curated, for the most part, for their factual content. In the 1950s, Wikipedia lists seven major music genres for North America: blues, classic pop, country music, folk, jazz, R&B, and rock and roll. The 1960s expands the number to eleven, adding roots rock, surf rock, blues rock, progressive rock, psychedelic rock, and garage rock. The subgenre "soul" now supplements R&B. By the 1970s, genres had diversified to include arena rock, punk, heavy metal, new wave, heavy metal, soft rock, and country rock. The Beatles were significant contributors to each of these major genres. By the 1990s, the site lists 18 major genres of music, and this expands further to 23 in the 2000s.

The Beatles, of course, were not the only band experimenting with these new styles and sounds. They were responsible for creating the niche markets that elevated bands and subgenres into the mainstream. They were an important catalyst by virtue of their ability to influence music tastes among a growing consumer base that was largely untapped and misunderstood by established industry leaders and executives.

But what were the Beatles doing that made this bet worth the risk?

A *Sgt. Pepper* deeper dive

The potentially revolutionary nature of the final product was not invisible to the producers or to EMI when the Beatles were recording *Sgt. Pepper's Lonely Hearts Club Band*. The album was a product of a well-established creative process, which had already demonstrated its commercial viability. *Rubber Soul* and *Revolver* had shown that the Beatles could monetize unconventional musical tastes and styles. Working with George Martin, they also had a keen sense for what types of songs would do well by charting and selling records. They had a well-earned track record for their success. While *Sgt. Pepper* was a departure, it was not completely out of left field. While McCartney and Lennon were pushing their art, the "revolution" was really part of an evolutionary and organic process. George Martin knew this well. "As I could see their talent growing," he recalled later in *All You Need Is Ears*, "I could recognize that an idea coming from them was better than an idea coming from me, though it would still be up to me to decide which was the better approach." Martin made a "tactical withdrawal" as he realized the Beatles' talent "was the greater talent."

Moreover, the first songs produced from the *Sgt. Pepper* sessions were singles, not contributions to the album. This allowed the Beatles, Martin, EMI, and Parlophone to gauge how the public would react to the music. "Strawberry Fields Forever," a distinctly psychedelic, art, progressive track, was released as an A-side single in February 1967, six months before the album dropped. The progressive, baroque pop, but less jarring "Penny Lane" were released as a second A-side to "Strawberry Fields." The two songs—among the best to be produced out of the *Sgt. Pepper* sessions and now classics in their own right—were, in effect, the "minimum viable product" to test the market. If these songs were commercial or critical flops, the album project might have been jeopardized as a commercial venture. EMI could afford a flop (even if Parlophone could not). The result would have simply relegated the Beatles to a niche market and undermined their broad appeal.

The *Sgt. Pepper* sessions were also structured sessions, providing an overall framework for directing their creative efforts. McCartney originally pitched the album as a "concept album"—a record with songs written to tell a story. While the ultimate product fell far short of what contemporaries would consider a true concept album—and was criticized heavily by Lennon at the time and after the breakup—many critics have argued the fundamental elements were there, at least in terms of content.

The original concept framed the *Sgt. Pepper Lonely Hearts Club Band* as the creative alter ego of the Beatles. The album starts out and ends with songs built around this idea. The Beatles use creative segues into different component parts of the songs to weave them together musically. Much of the content was also drawn from various elements of the Beatles' personal lives as well as milestones in any person's life. "She's Leaving Home" is a remarkably poignant story of a teenager leaving an emotionally oppressive home environment and the inability of her parents to grasp the reasons.

The iconic "A Day in the Life" pieces together snippets of one person's daily routine, including reproducing a "dream-like" state of consciousness that connects with the everyday work lives of many people. "A Day in the Life" is considered by many as the Beatles most creative and experimental song, introducing elements that had never been used before in pop music and rarely replicated since. The song includes three verses by Lennon, two orchestral crescendos, and middle part written and sung by McCartney. The first crescendo links the first verses by Lennon to the section crafted by McCartney. The orchestra, conceived by McCartney, included 40 musicians from the Royal Philharmonic Orchestra playing 24 bars arranged by Martin. The song ends with a dramatic simultaneous piano chord played on three pianos and a harmonium.

For all its progressive elements, *Sgt. Pepper's Lonely Hearts Club Band* is probably best understood stylistically by the stunning diversity of the songs, the intentionality behind the selection, and their organization. The album opens up with a simulation of a concert, introducing Sgt. Pepper's Lonely Hearts Club Band with guitars, horns, and other instruments, then introducing Billy Shears as a segue into Ringo Starr's "With a Little Help from My Friends." These songs are somewhat conventional pop-rock songs, up tempo with good rhythms. The third song is the psychedelic rock, acid rock "Lucy in the Sky with Diamonds." While the song was inspired by drawings by Lennon's son Julian of his friend Lucy literally in the sky with diamonds, the band's experimentation with drugs (including LSD) is credited with providing much of the imagery. The fourth song on side one is a more conventional tune: the upbeat pop rock song "Getting Better." This is followed by a similarly well-crafted but reflective, moderate tempo pop-rock song "Fixing a Hole." The sixth song is the ballad "She's Leaving Home." Side one of the album ends with the carnival and music-hall inspired "Being for the Benefit of Mr. Kite," which also incorporates sound collages.

Side two is musically more eclectic and adventurous, beginning with "Within You Without You," a George Harrison contribution inspired by Indian classical music. This is followed by "When I'm Sixty Four," written by Paul McCartney when he was sixteen. This song draws stylistically on popular musical hall, almost Vaudevillean, sounds. But the song carries a serious message about aging and relationships. The third song is "Lovely Rita," a paean to blue-collar relationships about a working-class guy trying to woo a meter maid. The fourth song is another upbeat song inspired by a very conventional domestic event—cornflakes for breakfast—"Good Morning, Good Morning." The song is noted for its changing time signatures. The album closes out with a reprise of "Sgt. Pepper's Lonely Hearts Club Band" and a song which has probably established itself as the epitome of the Beatles' willingness to experiment and push the envelope: "A Day in the Life."

In short, while *Sgt. Pepper's Lonely Hearts Club Band* is now recognized as one of the most path-breaking albums in pop music, the album's contribution in pop music history is more than the sum of its parts. While many of the songs are stylistically similar, each song has its own place on the album and contributes something different within its own genre. Most importantly of all, the album was a stunning commercial success. The album spent 27 weeks at the top of the UK album charts and 15 weeks at the top of the US album charts. The album won four Grammy awards and was the first rock LP to win Album of the Year.

Implications for popular culture

In sum, the Beatles were at an important point in their careers when they decided to stop touring in 1966. Riding a wave of a dramatically expanded consumer base of youth, largely ignored by the mainstream entertainment industry, the Beatles redefined popular music. After just four years of touring—less time than they spent honing their skills as musicians in Liverpool and Hamburg—they had become the wealthiest pop music artists in the world. Their experience was the quintessential example of identifying, exploiting, and expanding a new market. Their influence was the equivalent of the iPod of the 1960s.

Savvy record label executives in the US (at Capital Records) and in the UK (Parlophone) quickly noticed the power of the expanding consumer market once the success of the Beatles became evident. As the four Liverpudlians climbed the programs during their UK concert tours, eventually eclipsing American stars like Roy Orbison, the British Invasion of pop music began in earnest. The Beatles, among the earliest of the industry disruptors, amassed significant wealth. This wealth, in turn, gave them unheard of independence as creators. EMI executives were willing to ride the wave and trust what the Beatles would produce would be commercially successful.

More importantly, the Beatles leveraged their wealth to innovate. Their growth mindset allowed them to be inspired by other artists as well as push the frontiers of pop music more generally. Their sense of what was commercially marketable and willingness to invest in their industry (through the studio) created an ever expanding platform for other artists. Indeed, the Beatles as individuals and a group interacted well with other artists, writing songs for them as well as (later) providing a business platform for them to create their own music.

In retrospect, private markets and entrepreneurial capitalism were essential to their success as a band. These economic conditions, however, were not necessarily a sufficient condition for their continued success. For this, we turn to Chapter 5 and apply an economic framework to understand why the Beatles broke up, despite their commercial and artistic success as a band.

References

Carlson, Elwood. 2008. *The Lucky Few: Between the Greatest Generation and the Baby Boom.* New York: Springer.

Emerick, Geoff and Howard Massey. 2006. *Here, There, and Everywhere: My Life Recording the Music of the Beatles.* New York: Gotham Books.

Martin, George. 1994. *All You Need Is Ears: The Inside Personal Story of the Genius Who Created the Beatles*. New York: St. Martin's Griffin.

Turner, Steve. 2009. *The Beatles: A Hard Day's Write—The Stories Behind Every Song*. New York: MJF Books.

US Bureau of Labor Statistics. 1980. *Profile of Teenage Workers*. Bulletin 2039. Washington, DC: US Department of Labor.

US Census Bureau. 2002. *Demographic Trends in the 20th Century*. Washington, DC: US Census Bureau. Retrieved from www.census.gov/prod/2002pubs/censr-4.pdf, last accessed January 18, 2020.

World Bank. 2018. *World Development Indicators*. Washington, DC: World Bank.

5

BREAKING UP IS HARD TO DO ... OR IS IT?

Economic concepts: Optimal firm size, institutional constraints, innovation, entrepreneurship, path dependence, transaction costs, uncertainty, strategic judgement

Perhaps one of the most controversial and perplexing parts of Beatles history, at least for fans, is the break-up. The band was beginning to fray at the seams in late 1967 and the *White Album* sessions during the summer and fall of 1968 put their conflicts on full display to their studio collaborators. This is also the period when Ringo Starr briefly left the group. The group dynamic didn't improve with the "Get Back" sessions, which eventually became the *Let It Be* album released in May 1970. As the group re-formed in EMI's studios for the *Abbey Road* sessions, tensions seemed to give way to collegiality and creativity. Yet, within eight months of the album's release, and one month before their final album (*Let It Be*) was released, the Beatles had officially, permanently, and publicly split up. What happened?

Thousands of words have been devoted to explaining the break-up of the most successful pop music act in the world, but the perspective of economics may still shed some light, or clarity, on the causes and consequences of the break-up. The following section builds on the previous chapters to put the group's split into context. Subsequent sections will use the insights of transaction costs, principal–agent theory, and the economic theory of the firm to explain why the break-up was logical, could be anticipated, and, in the end, beneficial for the members and pop music more generally.

When coming together can't get you back

Seeds of the split seemed to be apparent almost as soon as the *Sgt. Pepper* album project had wrapped up. The next projects for the band were a contractual obligation to write the soundtrack for the movie *Yellow Submarine* and a McCartney-conceived movie soundtrack for *Magical Mystery Tour*. By all accounts, the Beatles approached the *Yellow Submarine* project as a business transaction, not a creative enterprise. They recorded six songs, but only two of them—"All Together Now" and "Hey Bulldog"—were recorded specifically for the album. The title song, "Yellow Submarine," had already been released as a single in 1966 and included on *Revolver*. George Harrison's "Only a Northern Song" was recorded during the *Sgt. Pepper* sessions but rejected for the album. *Magical Mystery Tour* was a more significant creative endeavor, a commercial and artistic success, producing influential songs such as "Magical Mystery Tour," "I am the Walrus" and "Fool on the Hill." The project was conceived by McCartney and includes contributions firmly in line with their psychedelic phase of song writing. The fractures in the group that ultimately led to its demise, however, are more fully seen in the sessions leading up to their next major album project: *The Beatles*, also known as the *White Album*.

Recorded over the summer and early fall of 1968, and released in November as a double album, the *White Album* was released with 30 tracks, and easily captures the title as the most experimental of their work. The vinyl discs include classic rock songs such as George Harrison's "While My Guitar Gently Weeps," rockers such as "Revolution" and "Back in the USSR," and what many consider one of the earliest contributions to what would become heavy metal or hard rock: "Helter Skelter." Written by Paul McCartney, "Helter Skelter" was explicitly designed to push the boundaries of rock in response to the Who's song "I Can See for Miles." The phrase "helter skelter" has become so iconic it now refers colloquially to a disorderly activity, event, or action, but was taken from an amusement park attraction. John Lennon's "Happiness is a Warm Gun," inspired by an issue of the magazine *American Rifleman* in the Abbey Road studio office, has become an iconic cover song for other bands, recognized for its complexity and craftsmanship.

The album, however, has numerous tracks that could be considered purely experimental and nonsensical. "Revolution 9," for example, is a sound collage with overlays of street noises and vocals from Lennon, Yoko Ono, and producer George Martin. "Wild Honey Pie" is fifty-two seconds of repetition of the title to the vaudeville-esque, music hall sound that frames "Honey Pie." The lyrics to George Harrison's "Savoy Truffle" were inspired by a box of chocolates.

At the same time, the *White Album* includes a number of artful, poignant songs. "Julia" is a heartfelt tribute to his mother, who abandoned him to his Aunt Mimi as a young child and then was killed in a car accident just as they were reconnecting in his teens. Paul McCartney's "Blackbird" is known for the complexity of its guitar work (inspired by Johann Sebastian Bach's "Bourrée in E minor").

McCartney now attributes the inspiration for the lyrics to the plight of black women in the United States in the wake of Martin Luther King, Jr's assassination during the American civil rights movement.

The vast breadth and diversity of the album is extraordinary and testimony to the productivity of the Beatles as a group. Many of the songs were written or inspired during their stay in India, studying under Maharishi Mahesh Yogi. By some accounts, the band wrote 40 songs during their months in India. Afterward, more than two dozen songs were recorded in rough forms at George Harrison's home before being taken into the studio. Thus, despite the conflict evident in the recording studios during the *White Album* sessions, the project began as inspired collaboration.

The sessions, however, quickly became marred by conflict. Several observers, including George Martin, noted that the *White Album* sessions provided the first glimpses of the band moving in individual directions, writing and recording separately. Individual members were feeling marginalized as well. Ringo Starr quipped that his playing time was so limited during the *Sgt. Pepper* sessions he learned "to play chess while we were recording it." Now, during the *White Album* sessions, Ringo was being marginalized while his drumming was being critiqued. In August, he left the band in frustration. He was coaxed back after cajoling from Lennon and McCartney.

But the seeds of tensions had been sowed earlier. Lennon was now in a personal relationship with Yoko Ono, and her presence in the studio disrupted the creative flow for the band. Lennon relied on her input during the creative process. This further distanced him from Paul McCartney. Rather than writing together, they often would develop work independently (although still relying on each other to "finish" their songs). Phil Norman, writing in *Shout!*, characterizes the relationship as so conflicted they were developing a disdain and aversion to each other's style of music. Sound engineer Geoff Emerick, who had been working with the Beatles since *Revolver* in 1966, left the band in July because he found the work environment toxic and unproductive. Notably, only sixteen of the thirty tracks have all four Beatles recording on them.

In the aftermath of the *White Album* sessions, Paul McCartney took the initiative to try something different to quell the discord. McCartney suggested they film the recording sessions for their next album, capping the process off with a live performance. These sessions would be known as the "Get Back" sessions, but the songs would not be released until after *Abbey Road* in 1969. The result, unfortunately, seemed to heighten tensions and drive the band even further apart. In retrospect, the very structure of the "Get Back" recording sessions seemed to work against the creative dynamic of the Beatles. The hours for recording were unusual for the Beatles since they had to accommodate the film crew. They were up early and done in late afternoon. They could no longer write spontaneously, or engage organically in marathon recording sessions. Indeed, when the *Let It Be* film was finally released, one month after McCartney's public declaration that he had left the Beatles, the public narrative was focused on the conflict and bickering between the bandmates. The famous rooftop concert was a compromise and spontaneous event, partially driven by the need to fulfill the requirements of the contract.

Paradoxically, the *Abbey Road* sessions (which immediately followed the "Get Back" sessions) were significantly more congenial. Both studio engineers and the bandmates noted an environment that was more conducive to creativity. In part, the sessions were structured to bring the band back to a more traditional recording approach that linked them to their past. The album includes creative banter among the bandmates. The songs were generally less technologically driven and stylistically more suitable to live performances. (An exception being the techno-progressive-psychedelic "Because," which triple tracked the vocals and used a Moog synthesizer and harpsichord.) McCartney's bluesy, doo-wop "Oh! Darling" has a powerful, soulful simplicity that also stretched his vocal skills. George Harrison's "Something" and "Here Comes the Sun" have become enduring classics, considered some of the best pop songs ever recorded.

Yet, eight months later, the Beatles were no longer a band, and the prospects for reconciling were remote, at best.

Dissolution economics

Of course, many historians, musicologists, colleagues, and peers have theories for why the band broke up. How can economics provide any additional insight into the end?

Surprisingly, for some, economics can help connect several dots and explain some of the key dynamics that led to the break-up. The Beatles, as an enterprise, may well be an example of business that simply ran its course and was unable to adjust to the changing economic, political, and cultural dynamics of its market. To some extent, these effects are evident in the interpersonal relationships of the Beatles. Each was going in their own direction, artistically, and the Beatles was simply too small and focused of a tent to hold their creativity. The Beatles were contractually obligated (under EMI) to produce two albums a year. When Apple Music was formed, these relationships and contracts were carried over. But the four Beatles were producing far greater product than could be contained in such a limited obligation. Only the "best" songs were making it onto the album, but given the space limitations, and the creative control exercised by Lennon and McCartney, many great songs were not seeing the light of day. Moreover, as the individual tastes diverged, songs that might be "great" within a particular genre would not necessarily compete effectively for the limited space on a Beatles album intended for their main and most general audience.

Perhaps no other example of this is as evident as George Harrison's success in the immediate aftermath of the break-up. His three-album set *All Things Must Pass*— his third overall but first since the break-up—contained twenty-three songs and was released in 1970. The recording session produced another double album's worth of material that wasn't issued. Harrison estimated he had a backlog of nearly 200 songs that had accumulated during his time with the Beatles. Despite the long list of Beatles rejections, the album went to the top and remained on the album charts in the UK and US (*Billboard, Cash Box*, and *Record World*). Moreover, in testimony to the good will Harrison had in the music world, more than 28 musicians collaborated in the production of these songs, including Ringo Starr, guitarists Eric Clapton and Peter Frampton, keyboardists Billy Preston and Gary Wright, progressive rock drummer Alan White, and several top session artists.

But Harrison's talents had grown beyond songwriting. Harrison was a prodigious collaborator and producer. He co-wrote Ringo Starr's post-Beatles hit song "It Don't Come Easy," co-wrote and produced his number one (US) hit "Back Off Boogaloo," and co-wrote the number one (US) hit "Photograph." He also organized the Concert for Bangladesh, considered the world's first global rock benefit concert, featuring supergroups and international superstars such as Bob Dylan, Eric Clapton, Badfinger, and others. For his part, Ringo Starr was engaged in a series of projects that would be critically acclaimed or well received, including an album of pre-rock classics (*A Sentimental Journey*) and a country album (*Beaucoups of Blues*).

Clearly, the problem faced by the Beatles was not a lack of talent. Rather, the band was faced with two potential problems that were embedded in its organization. By establishing Lennon and McCartney as the creative gatekeepers, they tended to favor their own tastes and preferences. This became particularly acute, and evident, during the *White Album* and "Get Back" sessions, where Lennon and McCartney bickered over style and artistic merit. As their tastes and interests diverged, their ability to objectively judge the value of the contributions others in the band became more tenuous.

The band was "path dependent" on the organizational structure of the band. As economists Martin Stack and Myles Gartland explain, the theory behind path dependency argues that "sub-optimal or inefficient technologies can become locked in as industry standards, and in instances where there are significant network effects, these inefficiencies can persist for extended periods of time" (Stack and Gartland 2003: 487). These effects can also occur at the level of the firm, or organization. The creative process of the Beatles, however, was locked in. Harrison and Starr had little opportunity to create outside this structure unless they produced their own solo recordings. George Harrison's experimental soundtrack to the film *Wonderwall*, released in 1968, may be one of the most significant examples of the constraining effect of the band. *Wonderwall Music* was the first solo album released by a Beatle and the first album produced and released by Apple Music.

George Harrison was not the only Beatle who felt stifled by the organizational structure of the band. Lennon and McCartney were also engaged in significant solo projects. McCartney's solo album, *Paul McCartney*, became a touchstone for the band's break-up when he refused to change the release date to accommodate the much delayed *Let It Be* album. Similarly, John Lennon was actively engaged in his own solo projects, having released the experimental albums *Unfinished Music No. 1: Two Virgins* in 1968, and *Unfinished Music No. 2: Life with the Lions* and *Wedding Album* in 1969. Their hit album *John Lennon/Plastic Ono Band* was released seven months after the band's official break-up in 1970.

The alternative, as Stack and Gartland point out, is to establish an opportunity for "path creation." A critical element of accomplishing this is to establish a strategic management team that recognizes the opportunities each team member can bring into the production process. Drawing on the concepts introduced in Chapter 3, these teams have to recognize the "heterogeneity" of the human capital on the team. Each of the team members brings elements into the innovation and production process (Foss et al. 2008). The management team—Lennon and McCartney in this case—have to establish a mindset that evaluates these contributions effectively. In addition, team dynamics need to ensure that each member can bring their knowledge, experience, and perspective into the equation.

When working effectively, the entrepreneurship team "can be as effective as the creative inputs provided by its members, which can expand and be enriched when members learned from each other's diverse ideas, perceptions, and expectations" (Foss et al. 2008: 83). The work of David Livermore, author of *Driven by Difference* and *Leading with Cultural Intelligence*, documents the benefits of this strategy through the work of the Cultural Intelligence Center. In the case of the Beatles, these effects could be seen in the disillusionment of George Harrison and the frustration of Ringo Starr. As Nicolai Foss and his colleagues note: "Capacities of human resources can neither be fixed nor scientifically engineered, although organizational conditions in which the human resources are embedded substantially influence these capacities" (Foss et al. 2008: 85).

To some degree, both George Harrison and Ringo Starr implicitly recognized the importance of this dynamic. George Harrison, for example, brought Eric Clapton into the *White Album* sessions and Billy Preston into the "Get Back" sessions as a tactic for calming the tension and conflict. Bringing strangers into the room, Harrison later recalled, changed the interpersonal dynamic because people want to be on their best behavior. Since the so-called strangers were also top-flight musicians—Preston had been backing their idol Little Richard when they first met and Clapton's guitar work was well recognized—they added a creative dimension that also allowed the band to pull together. Clapton's lead guitar contribution to one of Harrison's iconic Beatles songs, "While My Guitar Gently Weeps," is considered a virtuoso performance.

Blaming Lennon and McCartney on the negative dynamics during the *White Album* and "Get Back" sessions, however, appears to be short-sighted. Indeed, during the *Abbey Road* sessions, most observers recognized a positive dynamic had returned to the recording studio. Both Lennon and McCartney praised Harrison's contributions for perhaps contributing the best additions to the album. Organizational dynamics, however, are just one part of the story of the break-up. Another part is the fact their wealth and influence in the pop world made it easy for the band to break up and avoid resolving their differences.

The transaction costs of breaking up

Beyond the internal band dynamics, which triangulated around personality as well as differences in creative perspective, personal wealth played another important role. All the Beatles were independently wealthy. In fact, Apple Corps was set up January 1968, six months after the release of *Sgt. Pepper's Lonely Hearts Club Band* and one month after the release of *Magical Mystery Tour*, on the advice of their accountants, who were looking for a tax haven. English tax laws favored business ventures over personal income. The Beatles were in the nation's highest tax bracket, with marginal tax rates of around 90 percent, and the government was proposing a supercharge that would take it to 95 percent. Thus, for an individual, each additional dollar of personal income would be taxed at 95 percent, inspiring the opening lines "Let me tell you how it will be / There's one for you, nineteen for me / 'Cause I'm the taxman, yeah, I'm the taxman," in George Harrison's sardonic song "Taxman" on the *Revolver* album (1966).

The establishment of Apple Corps replaced their partnership (Beatles Ltd.) and, at least in theory, gave them greater creative control and more artistic opportunities in other fields such as film, electronics, publishing, retail, and recording. Originally conceived as a cooperative venture, the sprawling nature of the company, lack of corporate vision, and loose management style (requiring approval from individual Beatles in practice) compromised its ability to operate efficiently and effectively. One of the principal architects of the new entity was long-time manager Brian Epstein, who envisioned a chain of retail shops. The retail side of the company was short lived, perhaps because of Epstein's untimely and unexpected death in December 1967. Allen Klein took over the role of Apple Corps head when he was hired as the band's manager (over the strident objections of Paul McCartney). While Klein imposed some order to the business, his tenure as manager and executive was controversial. Long-time (and trusted) road manager Neil Aspinall took over the chief executive role and managed the company from 1970 to 2007.

While the company discovered, developed, and promoted several notable artists—James Taylor, Mary Hopkin, and Billy Preston, to name a few—most of the other divisions languished and the company became mired in lawsuits (most famously with Apple Inc., the computer firm). The film side of the business was also active, producing *Yellow Submarine, Magical Mystery Tour*, and *Let It Be* while the group was still together. Apple Corps, however, never evolved into the influential media company the Beatles had envisioned, eventually settling into managing Beatles solo projects and licensing various Beatles media products.

The band, however, was already disintegrating, as the recording sessions were demonstrating. The trials and tribulations of Apple Corps were both structural and an indicator of the shifting preferences and desires of the individual band members. As the strategic function of the team began to break down, and the organizational structure of the band no longer served the needs of the artists, the incentives for each individual band member to leave the group increased. Coupled with the greater incentives to leave was the dramatically lower cost of leaving the group.

Paradoxically, the most important decision the band made that enabled their experimental phase was also the one that effectively enabled the band to break up.

The Beatles had established its reputation and earned its wealth as a performance band. Beginning in the mid-1950s when John Lennon established the Quarrymen, the bandmates built their audience around honing their skills and widening their audiences on stage. "Beatlemania" was in full swing by the time the band broke into the American market in January 1964. With the charting of "Love Me Do" in 1962, the group's UK tours were characterized by audiences so loud that their music could barely be heard. The crescendo (and public attention) had become so overwhelming for the band that they decided to quit touring just four years later and just two years after entering the US market.

While the decision to stop touring released the band to dive deeper into its creative side, the consequence was also to lessen their dependence on each other. As they stretched the boundaries of the studio, including using their wealth to block out substantial time in the studio, largely independent of cost considerations, individual musicians could record at their own time and pace. As recording technology expanded from four-track to eight-track, the need for other band members to record together was lessened even further.

Touring put inherent pressure on the band to stay together, for financial as well as artistic reasons. In the early years, performances helped each member of the band improve their skills, rotate personnel to find the right mix, and create a unique sound that could connect to their fans—the consumers of their music. The band, as an entity, created a mechanism for them to monetize the artistic value created in their efforts through markets. This was particularly important because rock and roll was not recognized as a commercially viable art form in 1950s England.

Even in the US, rock music was considered a niche market with little broad appeal during the Beatles' formative years. Rooted in country music and rhythm and blues, the genre had yet to coalesce and spread to a broader mainstream audience until the middle of the 1950s. Bill Haley and the Comets released their first rock and roll hit "Crazy Man, Crazy" in 1953, and African American blues artist Big Joe Turner released "Shake, Rattle and Roll" in 1954. Unfortunately, most African American rhythm and blues artists remained in niche markets, at times finding more success in Europe than in the US. The US market did not begin to mature until after Elvis Presley's breakout hit "Heartbreak Hotel," which was released in 1956 (the year the Quarrymen were formed). Buddy Holly's classic "That'll Be the Day" didn't top the charts until 1957 (the year Paul McCartney joined the Quarrymen).

The residencies in Hamburg were critical to their development as a band. They improved their skills as performers and musicians, but they were also paid. Eventually, as their brand became better known, they would be able to tour and monetize their artistic contributions. Once they had sufficient notoriety and a large enough fan base they could attract the attention of record companies (the ultimate goal of bands in that period). Even with their success in Hamburg and in northern England, they needed an entrepreneurial producer to sign them (which they found in George Martin at Parlophone records). Even with their success in England, Capitol Records, who owned EMI and Parlophone, was still skeptical of their commercial viability. The North American tour only happened after their success in the UK, dubbed Beatlemania by the press, convinced promoters and recording professionals in America that they could be a hit. Thus, the band, and touring in particular, were critical to establishing their commercial viability and generating the wealth necessary to allow for musical experimentation. The Beatles' work on *Rubber Soul* and *Revolver* demonstrated the commercial and artistic viability of studio work, at least as it applied to the group.

The success of *Sgt. Pepper* fundamentally changed this organizational and business dynamic. Very few of the songs produced during the *Sgt. Pepper* sessions could be played live with the technology of the time. The full orchestra used for "A Day in the Life" could only be reproduced on stage at significant cost to hire and rehearse with classical musicians. The iconic detail of the piccolo flute would not be cost-effective in concert, either, except under special circumstances. Of course, "Lucy in the Sky with Diamonds" and "Strawberry Fields" owed their success to in-studio innovations that could also not be reproduced easily or effectively on stage (although they could be covered by other musicians in less complex and technology-driven ways).

Without the pressure of the live tours, the Beatles also had more time to create on their own. They could experiment with different technologies, different arrangements, and simply increase the volume of the songs they could write. The exacting process of culling music to curate the best songs for the albums meant that large caches of music were left buried on tapes or deferred to future projects.

The ability to spend more time in the studio, combined with the luxury of experimentation guaranteed by their wealth, meant that the band could explore different versions of songs, whether it was a blues-rock version of "Revolution" or "Helter Skelter" or a sound collage. The number of takes during the recording process increased steadily, from just a few when they were reproducing songs played on stage to dozens for songs with more complex structures. Naturally judgements about the quality of the work produced (and distributed) varied by individual tastes and preferences. As John Lennon was exploring more experimental music with Yoko Ono, Paul McCartney was continuing to develop melodic songs and expanding his own music skill set, George Harrison continued to invest in Indian-inspired styles and Phil Specter-inspired "wall of sound" arrangements, and Ringo Starr felt the pull of performance. The individual members found the benefits of staying in the band were less and less, and the costs were higher and higher.

The art marches on

Importantly, in the studio, the members could come together and produce high-quality music. While *Abbey Road* was released in 1969 to mixed reviews, the album is now considered one of their finest. The album, with George Martin as lead producer, reflects a maturity in content and production quality lacking in previous albums.

Overall, the music on the albums released in 1968, 1969, and 1970 reflects a stylistic balance that differentiates this period from previous eras. Conventional wisdom splits the Beatles' recording era into two periods: a rock and roll era (from 1962 to 1966) and an experimental and progressive era (1967 to 1970). A more fine-grained analysis of their music suggests three periods. The first period, from 1962 to 1964, is characterized by their touring phase. This is the era where they established their fan base and the commercial value of the band on a national (UK) and global scale. The band entered a distinctly experimental phase during the three-year period spanning 1965 and 1967. The band expanded their artistic range through innovation in the studio as they continued to push the envelope on a wide range of music and musical styles. This is the period that saw the release of *Rubber Soul, Revolver,* and *Sgt. Pepper's Lonely Hearts Club Band.*

An analysis of the final three years of the band's existence, however, reveals a more complex period, where their music is balanced between experimental and traditional rock and roll/R&B. These are the albums where experimental music coexists with classic rock and pop music. This is the period that includes the *White Album* as well as *Magical Mystery Tour, Abbey Road,* and *Let It Be.*

The stylistic and musical balance reflected in the final albums have led some commentators to wistfully wonder what "would have been" if the Beatles had stayed together. Given the well-crafted and polished nature of the music on these final recordings, perhaps the band could have produced even more work of such a

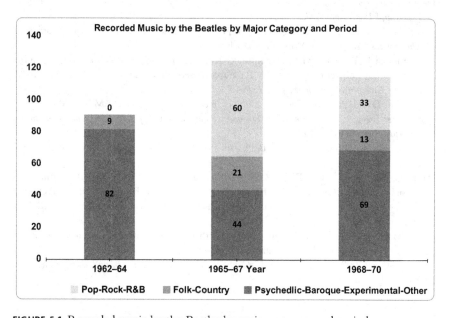

FIGURE 5.1 Recorded music by the Beatles by major category and period
Source: Created by the author from Wikipedia, "List of Songs Recorded by the Beatles," last accessed by author June 25, 2019

high caliber if they could have resolved their personal differences (without the distractions of the legal troubles associated with Apple Corps). Others have suggested that *Abbey Road*, which reflected the last sessions where the Beatles recorded together, was a "swan song," a final send-off before they broke up.

An economic view suggests a different interpretation. Rather than view *Abbey Road* as a swan song, or the inevitable result of a clash of personalities, their final music reflects the limits of what the bandmates could achieve together under one entity. The band no longer provided the creative context necessary for them to move forward as artists and creators. The very structure of the band, and its associated path dependence, meant that the only way they could continue to create would be to split up and develop their own solo careers. This is the subject of the final chapter.

Before moving to that chapter, however, to what extent does this economic framework apply to other bands? A small, but important digression to examine the career and impacts of other bands emerging at the same time as the Beatles helps provide insight into the robustness of the economic view of pop music bands. The next chapter uses these ideas and concepts to take a new look at the Beatles' most important economic competitors: the Rolling Stones and the Beach Boys.

References

The Beatles. 2000. *The Beatles: Anthology*. London: Apple Corps.

David, Paul. 1985. "Clio and the Economics of QWERTY." *American Economic Review, Papers and Proceedings*, 75(5), 332–337.

Emerick, Geoff and Howard Massey. 2006. *Here, There and Everywhere: My Life Recording the Music of the Beatles*. New York: Gotham Books.

Foss, Nicolai J., Peter G. Klein, Yasemin Y. Kor, and Joseph T. Mahoney. 2008. "Entrepreneurship, Subjectivism, and the Resource-Based View: Toward a New Synthesis." *Strategic Entrepreneurship Journal*, 2, 73–94.

Livermore, David. 2015. *Leading with Cultural Intelligence*. New York: AMACOM.

Livermore, David. 2016. *Driven by Difference: How Great Companies Fuel Innovation through Diversity*. New York: AMACOM.

Norman, Philip. 2003. *Shout! The Beatles in their Generation*, revised edition. New York: Fireside Books.

Rutledge-Borger, Meredith E. 2012. "Billy Preston has the Distinction of Being the Only Musician besides the Band Members to Be Credited on a Beatles Record." Retrieved from www.rockhall.com/how-billy-preston-helped-beatles-get-back, last accessed September 30, 2019.

Stack, Martin and Myles P. Gartland. 2003. "Path Creation, Path Dependency, and Alternative Theories of the Firm." *Journal of Economic Issues*, 37(2), 487–494.

Turner, Steve. 2009. *The Beatles: A Hard Day's Write—The Stories Behind Every Song*. New York: MJF Books.

6

A SECOND COMING?

Lessons from the Rolling Stones and the Beach Boys

Economic concepts: Heterogeneous capital, diminishing marginal returns, entrepreneurial judgement

The 1960s were a turbulent period, culturally and politically, throughout the Western Hemisphere, particularly in Europe and the United States. The massive post-World War II wealth created by peace led to an economic juggernaut driven by teenagers, young adults, and professionals with relatively large amounts of spendable cash. Post-war generations were pushing against the constraints of traditional Western society, exercising their voice to influence a wide range of institutions, political as well as cultural. They were also pushing the boundaries of cultural decorum.

The Beatles entered this cauldron of social change at the earliest stages—too young to be tarred by the memories of the war but old enough to push boundaries through their actions and decisions. They were Elwood Carlson's "lucky few." The effect was unexpected, at least among those at the very beginning. The record industry had pushed pop music into the background, unable to see how the Baby Boomers were pushing the boundaries of taste. Indeed, the Beatles' initial personal interests were quite modest: a hit record, enough money to continue as musicians, and, given the times, girls that come with teen idolatry. No one—producers, promoters, peers, or the Beatles themselves—believed their run as a commercially successful band would be long-term. Even when they were successful, the Beatles and their commercial supporters believed their careers as performers, like other pop musicians, would be short. When asked what they would do "after" Beatlemania, Lennon and McCartney both indicated they planned to be song writers. That was the business model in the 1950s; the real money was in writing songs that other artists would sing and producers would make popular.

Of course, the Beatles set new standards for being successful, transforming the industry. They undoubtedly would have continued to sustain much of their popularity and commercial success if they had stayed together. Earlier chapters used the economic lens to gain insight into why the Beatles were commercially and artistically successful. Can the same lens help understand why other groups (or solo acts) failed to have the same impact? The era of the 1960s and 1970s saw an explosion of music acts, some part of the British invasion (e.g., the Rolling Stones, the Who, Pink Floyd, Led Zeppelin, the Kinks, the Hollies, and others) and others from the United States (e.g., the Beach Boys, Creedence Clearwater Revival, Bob Dylan, the Byrds, the Temptations, the Supremes). Many of these bands were wildly successful, and many pioneered their genres. Why did these other bands with just as much potential as the Beatles fail to achieve similar levels of success and influence?

Space does not permit an extensive analysis of each of the bands in detail. However, a closer look at two globally influential bands in popular music—the Rolling Stones from the UK and the Beach Boys from the US—using the concepts introduced in earlier chapters to explore their dynamic and influence can help draw insight into the enduring success of the Beatles. Previous chapters suggested that the Beatles' success was not all serendipity. Their success was also far from preordained. They had to intentionally make decisions that put themselves in positions to take advantage of opportunities as they emerged onto the national and then international pop music scene. But so did other groups. If the lens of economics is helpful in understanding the rise and sustainable success of the Beatles, and their break-up, perhaps a similar perspective can provide insight into why other groups (and individual artists) fell short of achieving the same level of influence.

The Rolling Stones

The Rolling Stones were formed in 1962 after original bandmates Mick Jagger, Brian Jones, and Keith Richards moved into an apartment together in London. They had just graduated from the US equivalent of high school, and Mick Jagger was studying at the London School of Economics. The group's first performance occurred on July 1962, just a few months before the Beatles recorded their first hit single "Love Me Do" and in between their third and fourth Hamburg residencies. Like the Beatles, the Rolling Stones played for free as they developed their skills, sharpened their style, and started to build a fan base. Their first live performance tour was also in 1962.

Despite their modest beginnings, the Rolling Stones' star rose quickly. In fact, it rose much more quickly than the Beatles. By the time the Beatles had their first record deal, they had been playing together for nearly five years. Yet, just two years after the Rolling Stones formed, some polls ranked their popularity higher than the Beatles in England. The Stones' first US hit—"(I Can't Get No) Satisfaction"—climbed to the top of the US charts in 1965, three years after they had formed. Their song finished third at year-end, higher than the Beatles hit "Help!" (which ended up fifth). The Stones continued to chart near or at the top with songs such as "Paint It Black," "Honky Tonk Women," and "Brown Sugar."

Unlike the Beatles, the Stones have stayed together and continue to tour with their earliest core members from the 1960s intact—Mick Jagger (vocals), Keith Richards (guitar), Charlie Watts (percussion). They have sold more than 240 million albums (100 million "certified", about one-third of the sales of the Beatles), and three of the Stones' fifty tours rank among the highest-grossing of all time. The band was inducted into the Rock and Roll Hall of Fame in 1989, just one year after the Beatles and the Beach Boys. Lead guitarist and original band member Keith Richards is recognized as one of rock music's greatest guitarists of all time.

Yet, despite their accolades and massive commercial success, the Rolling Stones' influence has been less culturally and musically broad than the Beatles. Their impact within their genre, however, may well have been more profound. The economic theory of the firm introduced in Chapter 3 helps provide insight into why their influence was more narrow, more impactful in their genre, as well as why they have been more sustainable as a band.

The group dynamic within the Rolling Stones is quite complex and very different from the Beatles. Both bands (as well as the Beach Boys) were "self-contained" bands—they played their own instruments, wrote their own songs, and largely relied on themselves to produce their own music. In some important respects, the Rolling Stones were pushing faster and more innovatively than the Beatles within the pop music industry. The Rolling Stones signed with Decca in 1964, a major music label that had turned the Beatles down when Brian Epstein was shopping them to nearly two dozen mainstream record companies in 1962. Their manager also negotiated a significantly better business deal for the band—higher royalty rates, more access to recording studio time, and the flexibility to record in studios independent of Decca. (Notably, George Martin and others cite this treatment of the Beatles by their label, EMI, as one of the reasons that led to the formation of Apple Corps.) Mick Jagger continued to lead the band on the business side and is widely credited with navigating the Rolling Stones into very lucrative deals with Decca and other labels, particularly after the departure of their manager.

The Rolling Stones, however, suffered from poor group dynamics almost from the beginning. While the Beatles were a tight-knit set of friends who had bonded over their music through years touring northern England and living together in their residencies in Hamburg, the Rolling Stones were able to hitch on to the commercial success ignited by Beatlemania to ride the wave. The core of the early group—Brian Jones, Mick Jagger, Keith Richards, Dick Taylor, and Ian Stewart—began to falter early on. Taylor and Stewart left the group while Bill Wyman (bass guitar) joined in late 1962, and Charlie Watts (drums, percussion) was added to the line-up in early 1963. The band, however, quickly settled into a core group of four—Jones, Jagger, Richards, and Wyman—which then became Jagger, Richards, Wyman, and Mick Taylor after Brian Jones left in 1969. (Ronnie Wood replaced Mick Taylor in 1975, and Wyman left in 1993.) The turnover in "permanent" members, however, had the effect of consolidating control and influence within the band. Particularly after the departure of Jones, songwriting and creative control was concentrated in Jagger and Richards.

The Stones' popularity rose quickly: Their first single, a Chuck Berry cover of "Come On," almost cracked the top 20 in the UK when it was released in the summer of 1963. Their second single, the Lennon/McCartney song "I Wanna Be Your Man," also released in 1963, reached number twelve on the UK singles charts. Their third single, a cover of the Buddy Holly song "Not Fade Away," reached number three.

While the success of these singles allowed the Rolling Stones to break out of their London market and secure their first UK concert tour (supporting American rockers Bo Didley, Little Richard, and the Everly Brothers), their future lay in original music, not covers. Their first single as a Jagger/Richards composition ("Heart of Stone") was released in December 1964 and climbed into the top twenty in the US. Their second album, *Rolling Stones No. 2*, climbed to number one in January 1965. Now, they were also touring on a global scale, including concerts in Australia and New Zealand.

The Rolling Stones image and persona also developed in stark contrast to the Beatles. Their sound was more deeply rooted in blues and R&B, and their image was fashioned as part of the 1960s counter-culture—loud, artistically loose, irreverent, and unpredictable. This persona reflected a competitive positioning since the Rolling Stones needed to differentiate itself from the polished, tightly woven image, and creatively adventurous Beatles. But the Stones' image reflected their music as well, and plenty of room existed for both. As Richards explains in his memoir *Life*, regarding the Lennon and McCartney song written for the Stones that would become their first hit:

> [Lennon and McCartney] deliberately aimed [the song] at us. They're songwriters ... and they thought this song would suit us ... Mick and I admired their harmonies and their songwriting capabilities; they envied us our freedom of movement and our image.

In terms of influence, the impact of the Rolling Stones on rock music cannot be over-stated. The Rolling Stones' influence may well have defined the contemporary rock and roll genre. *Rolling Stone* magazine ranked them as the fourth "greatest" artist in rock music, right behind Elvis Presley (no. 3) and Bob Dylan (no. 2). The Beatles were ranked number one. (The next highest-ranked band, the Beach Boys, was ranked number twelve.) They were just the seventh band to be inducted into the Rock and Roll Hall of Fame. (The Everly Brothers and the Coasters were the first two.) Moreover, no other band competed more directly with, or in terms of influence, with the Beatles than the Rolling Stones as a foundational component of the so-called British invasion of the 1960s. While the Beatles may have started the invasion into popular music, the Rolling Stones amped up the impact.

In the late 1960s, however, the Rolling Stones took a stylistic detour that could have derailed the band permanently. In late 1967, the band released *Their Satanic Majesties Request*, a psychedelic album completely produced by the Stones. While the album was commercially successful (reaching number three in the UK and number two in the US), critics panned it. Coming on the heels of *Sgt. Pepper's Lonely Hearts Club Band*, and the earlier release of equally innovative *Pet Sounds* by the Beach Boys, *Satanic Majesties* appeared to many, particularly critics, as a cheaper, less interesting, and less innovative copy of the Beatles. The band separated from their manager, Andrew Loog Oldham, at this point as well. (While the circumstances appear to be somewhat murky and connected to off-stage controversies, the separation appeared to be amicable.)

Entrepreneurial judgement in the Rolling Stones

Fortunately, their next album, *Beggars Banquet*, released in 1968, would anchor the subsequent course of their career. Musically, the album re-grounded the group in blues, rock, and country music, and included the hit songs "Jumpin' Jack Flash" and "Sympathy for the Devil." By the beginning of 1970s, the band had released ten albums over just six years, which was somewhat lower output than the Beatles when they were formed. But music was changing. As the Beach Boys, the Beatles, and a few other bands began focusing on recording and studio production, no longer supporting concert tours, overall output began to fall. The Rolling Stones would go on to release another six albums in the 1970s, a still respectable effort, but just four during the decade of the 1980s.

The Rolling Stones' influence, while profound, has been largely contained within rock music. Some of their members (e.g., Brian Jones) experimented with exotic instruments, and various members, most notably Keith Richards, experimented with new sounds on their guitars, but the blues-driven rock sound has been its signature. Unlike the Beatles, which pushed the envelope on new sounds in multiple genres, the focus on guitar-heavy rock music reflected entrepreneurial judgement that best took advantage of the heterogeneous capital embedded in the unique talents of Mick Jagger, Keith Richards, Brian Jones, Ian Stewart, Mick Taylor, Bill Wyman, Ronnie Wood, and Charlie Watts.

Acclaimed rock guitarist Steven Van Zandt, writing for *Rolling Stone* magazine, compared the Stones to the Beatles:

> The Stones were alien and exciting, too. But with the Stones, the message was, "Maybe you can do this." The hair was sloppier. The harmonies were a bit off. And I don't remember them smiling at all. They had the R&B traditionalist's attitude: "We are not in show business. We are not pop music."

This characterization of their image also reflects the artistic genius of the Rolling Stones. Their success is testimony to the recognition that the band, rather than a solo act, was a key to their commercial and artistic success.

The prodigious production of rock songs from the Rolling Stones can be attributed to two critical components: the song-writing duo of Mick Jagger and Keith Richards and their near continuous touring over several decades. Artistically, their impact was most keenly felt during their first decade. Even Van Zandt acknowledges that "their power comes from their first 12 albums," with few "great songs since '72." The importance of these songs should not be underestimated, however. The power of those songs allowed the band to leverage their artistry into a lengthy career, continuing to build their fan base as they broadened their impact.

Nevertheless, Jagger and Richards stayed in "their lane"—blues-influenced rock music. By holding closer to their R&B and blues roots, they helped establish a gritty, raw, powerful form of a musical art even more expressive and energizing in live performances compared to studio albums. Thus, they pushed the boundaries of live performance art, even as they were less likely to challenge genres outside of their blues-based rock genre.

Indeed, Mick Jagger is recognized as perhaps the world's top rock stage performer and is the iconic image of the rock music front man. The Rolling Stones' popularity is built around their individual personalities and on-stage persona. Naturally, their songs lend themselves to live performances in their simplicity, style and power. In concert, "they're still able to communicate that original power," Van Zandt says. And, as their band bio for the Rock and Roll Hall of Fame notes:

> They've released a steady stream of archival album reissues and live releases, and ... Jagger is as spry and charismatic now as he was during the Stones' original heyday. The band's status as an unstoppable rock & roll machine remain uncontested.

Some might be tempted to diminish the Rolling Stones' impact relative to the Beatles—a versatile, musically dynamic band—based on these observations alone. Yet, the perspective of entrepreneurial judgement, and its role in fostering creative production and innovation, adds a new dimension to an assessment of the Rolling Stones' artistic and commercial impact. As in the case of the Beatles, the artists themselves are human capital assets which bring unique attributes into the enterprise. The question for the entrepreneur centers on the best way to utilize these assets to achieve the goals of the band. As in the case of the Beatles, a narrow focus on the songwriters risks underestimating the value and benefit of the other members of the band. Original member Brian Jones, and near original members Charlie Watts (on drums) and Bill Wyman (on bass guitar), were also central to forming the Rolling Stones sound and brand. Brian Jones, for example, played the signature sitar lines on their 1966 number one hit "Paint It Black." Their blues style, like the Beatles, was inspired and informed by a blend of genres that became foundational to an entirely new genre of music. Moreover, the stability of the core members is testimony to the importance of keeping a basic artistic sensibility and structure, keyed to the core components, to continue its success. As a result, the Rolling Stones influence penetrated deeper and with more complexity into the rock genre than the Beatles. They were capable of creating number one hits with ballads such as the 1973 hit "Angie" (which includes strings), but more often they would build in a contemporary sensibility to a blues and soul foundation as Bill Wyman's bass in their number one dance song "Miss You" (1978).

The importance of coalescing their artistic production around bandmates with similar musical sensibilities may be illustrated by the departure of the most experimental of the original members, Brian Jones. As a founding member, Jones was instrumental in leading the group toward more experimentation. When he left, the band experimented less and concentrated song writing even more heavily into Jagger and Richards. Jones was replaced by Mick Taylor, who played with the band until 1974. While a central figure, and perhaps the most melodic guitarist to play in the band, Taylor's legacy (much like Ringo Starr) is in his role as a musician focused on supporting the sound of the band and the songs written by others. In 1975, Ronnie Wood replaced Taylor in the line-up. Taylor and Wood played important roles in developing and maintaining a signature performance sound of the band—dueling guitars, playing off each other as well as in tandem.

In contrast to the relative longevity of the core group, other players remained on the periphery as contract musicians. Founding member and keyboardist Ian Stewart left the band in 1963 but continued to work with them on contract until his death in 1985. Seventeen musicians joined the Rolling Stones with regular roles as touring members of the band, but they were not members of the core band. Their peripheral roles meant their contributions were less central to developing and maintaining they brand, nor where their artistic contributions considered significant enough to influence their style.

These observations are less criticism of Jagger and Richards and more about how seriously and effectively they used artists as critical resources to be used to further the Rolling Stones. Like the Beatles, the Rolling Stones relied extensively on session musicians for their expertise and professionalism to produce the sound the band wanted to project. Some musicians, such as Mick Taylor, and to a lesser extent Ian Stewart, emerged as sufficiently critical to the band that they were retained as part of the permanent or semi-permanent line-up. The crucial point is that, as entrepreneurs, Jagger and Richards were assessing the quality of the resources at their disposal, when they were best used, and in what capacity they were used. By most accounts, however, Jagger and Richards have been both the driving force and the glue that keeps the band together to this day.

Another factor working in favor of the Rolling Stones was touring. As the discussion of the Beatles showed, once the band no longer toured, the benefits of keeping the band together diminished while the transactions costs associated with staying together increased as they pursued separate artistic directions. Given that the band's power dynamic centered on two partners, rather than four, the ability to identify a common focus and concentrate their resources on that goal was easier. As Keith Richards noted, the Rolling Stones had only one "front man"—Mick Jagger—while the Beatles had four (although he was probably under-estimating his role in the power duo). The Rolling Stones' emphasis on touring significantly raised the stakes for splitting up. While guitarists and keyboardists could come and go, the identity of the Rolling Stones was built around Mick Jagger's stage presence and Keith Richards's guitar work. In the case of the Rolling Stones, the benefits of staying together were much more significant.

The organizational dynamic reflected the importance of keeping the band focused on a more singular genre, albeit a creative and boundary pushing one within the genre. The band stayed together by embracing artists with similar musical tastes and preferences even when their personalities created destructive and toxic relationships. The feuds between Mick Jagger and Keith Richards are legendary in the pop music world. These disagreements led to protracted periods of low output and inactivity, particularly in the 1980s and 1990s. In the case of the Rolling Stones, the benefits to staying together as a band reflected the entrepreneurial judgements of the core band members, and, in the process, created significant social value and benefit by ensuring the band stayed together and stayed on tour. Thus, just as the economic lens could be used to understand why the Beatles broke up, it can provide a framework for understanding why the Rolling Stones continues as a band as a matter of artistic expression, production, and commerce.

Within the rock genre, the Rolling Stones are peerless. They defined a sound for a generation. As William Langley notes writing in *The Telegraph*, the rock and roll "business in the early 1960s was ramshackle and crooked, and came with a built-in assumption that no one was going to last in it for very long." Mick Jagger had a substantial role in changing the business model to shift compensation more in favor of the artist and, as a consequence, creating a sustainable business model.

The Beach Boys

Another useful but somewhat complex example of a band that had the potential to eclipse the Beatles is the case of the Beach Boys. Perhaps more than any other band, the Beach Boys did more to keep an American footprint in pop music in the 1960s, fending off quite successfully the British invasion. Like the Beatles and the Rolling Stones, the Beach Boys were riding a macroeconomic wave of an expanding base of consumers and rising disposable income. The Beach Boys had two other important competitive effects: they established a commercially successful mainstream genre alternative—"surf music"—and they were willing to experiment with sound and music structure. In terms of creativity and breadth of their artistic impact, the band came much closer to rivaling the Beatles than almost any other band.

Like the Rolling Stones, the Beach Boys were an early power band. The signed on to Capital Records earlier and charted top 10 hits earlier than the Beatles. Their upbeat music and unique blend of harmonies were a natural progression from the pop and lighter rock music making its way into mainstream US teen culture. More importantly, perhaps, their music was more completely nested in the newest wave of teen culture. The American public responded enthusiastically. The Beach Boys scored twenty top 40 hits before 1966, a critical year for their creativity and for pop music. Notably, the band was inducted into the Rock and Roll Hall of Fame during the same year as the Beatles.

The Beach Boys were formed in 1961 in southern California with the gifted musician and songwriter Brian Wilson as the hub. His brothers Dennis and Carl were added to the line up along with cousin Mike Love and high school friend Al Jardine to complete the band. Their harmonies gave them a signature sound that meshed well with the spry and spirited beat of surf music, defining a genre and generation. Their first number one hit came in 1963 with "Surfin' USA," followed by "I Get Around" in 1964 (the same year the Beatles "invaded" America with "I Want To Hold Your Hand"). They continued to compete for the number one spot in 1965 with the release of "Help Me Rhonda," which ended up eleventh overall at the end of 1965 on the Billboard Hot 100 year-end rankings. ("Help Me Rhonda" finished slightly lower than "Help!," which ranked seventh, and "(I Can't Get No) Satisfaction," which ended up third.)

What really gave the Beach Boys a run at the Beatles' legacy, however, was Brian Wilson's imaginative and ground-breaking work on *Pet Sounds*, their eleventh studio album, released in 1966. This album preceded *Sgt. Pepper's Lonely Hearts Club Band*—the Beatles' eighth studio album—and may well be credited as the first pop music LP that used the recording studio as an integral component of composing and producing music. Like the Beatles, Brian Wilson incorporated new instruments, orchestration, and sounds that simply had not been heard, or even tried, on a pop album. Wilson had stopped touring with the band so he could focus on the album in 1966, which also led to his first solo single ("Caroline, No"). Indeed, its influence is so significant that Rolling Stone ranked it the second "greatest" album of all time, second only to *Sgt. Pepper*. The Beatles album may have eclipsed *Pet Sounds* only because it sold more records.

The artistic connection between the Beach Boys and the Beatles was much more than casual. Brian Wilson has publicly acknowledged the role *Rubber Soul* played in inspiring him to invest in producing *Pet Sounds*. Similarly, the Beatles have acknowledged how the ambition of *Pet Sounds* inspired their own experimentation and adventurous songwriting on *Sgt. Pepper*. Moreover, Paul McCartney's rocking parody "Back in the USSR," the lead track on side one of *The Beatles* (the *White Album*), is an explicit nod to the artistry of Brian Wilson and the Beach Boys.

Despite the artistic brilliance of Brian Wilson, the Beach Boys faltered and nearly disappeared before their legacy could be fully cemented. The band continues to tour, and generate significant revenue, but its contemporary success is rooted in nostalgia and produces relatively little original material. Indeed, their induction into the Hall of Fame is based on their profound impact on the music scene and pioneering work in the early and mid-1960s. Brian Wilson's experimental and progressive follow up album, *Smile*, was not released until 2011 (as *The Smile Sessions*). A stripped down version of the recordings, *Smiley Smile* became their twelfth studio album, but performed poorly. (The album is now considered a cult classic.)

The primary reasons for the Beach Boys' decline are more intuitive than the economic case for the Beatles' break-up. Brian Wilson's descent into drug use and subsequent onset of mental illness in the late 1960s and early 1970s crippled his ability to work consistently. Wilson also dropped out from the band's touring in

1965 so he could concentrate on studio recording. The band continued to play, perpetuating its image as a cohesive artistic force, even as Wilson became more and more displaced from the band's work. Given Wilson's central role as the creative driver of the band, the artistic influence of the Beach Boys waned.

What can the economics lens add to this story? The case of the Beach Boys reinforces the economic framework developed in Chapter 3. Both transaction costs and entrepreneurial management help explain the artistic decline of the Beach Boys. Unlike the Beatles and the Rolling Stones, the Beach Boys' creative force was extracted from the live performances. The merging of the creative and performance elements were critical to the Beach Boys launch into the mainstream. While Brian Wilson served the role of the central figure as artistic entrepreneur, the band was also essential to carrying out this vision and translating it into commercial venues.

At the time—the late 1950s and early 1960s—pop music artists sustained themselves on their performances and studio recordings supported their concert tours. The band continued to play live performances, monetizing their creative contributions on the road. This wealth, as with the Beatles, allowed Brian Wilson to amass enough income to stop performing and spend a year developing new material, creating new sounds, and experimenting with unconventional compositions. Wilson achieved these feats largely by himself. When the Beach Boys returned from touring, they were inserted into the recording process as musicians rather than creators. The value of the band as an institutional framework for creating new music was largely severed.

The separation of Brian Wilson from the band weakened the creative benefits of the band, but created a more resilient structure for perpetuating the sounds it created. Indeed, as Brian Wilson's mental illness manifested itself, and his creative interests diverged from those of the rest of the band, his projects began to falter while the band was able to continue largely intact. Despite the global success (and influence) of "Good Vibrations," the costliest single produced at the time, Wilson's unwillingness to compromise and work with his fellow bandmates kept the even more musically ambitious album *Smile* unfinished. A stripped down and less well-produced version, *Smiley Smile*, was released in 1967 but peaked at just 41 on the US album charts (although rising to ninth in the UK). The Beach Boys were unable to reclaim their momentum as a creative force in pop music. After Carl Wilson took over the band as creative director, the Beach Boys continued to tour but failed to achieve the musical influence it had before 1967. In terms of their overall influence, this impact was profound enough for the band to become one of the earliest inductees into the Rock and Roll Hall of Fame.

Lessons learned

What does economic analysis suggest about the enduring legacy of the Beatles? More specifically, what does economic analysis suggest about whether another band could achieve the same level of influence or success?

All bands, of course, are faced with the similar challenge of optimizing the use of their heterogeneous human capital—the musicians, songwriters, producers, and technicians—for a common goal. The Beatles were important because they allocated their human capital in such a way that their internal organizational structure fostered innovation and was, for the most part, inclusive. While John Lennon and Paul McCartney bore the lion's share of the responsibility for ensuring the quality of the music the Beatles produced, their decision rules focused on the content of songs, not individuals. Even George Harrison recognized that his early songs were rejected for distribution on early Beatles albums because the quality and distinctiveness of his compositions did not reach the high standards established by the band.

Harrison and Ringo Starr, however, were integral members of the band and continued to make artistic contributions. While John Lennon wrote "Norwegian Wood," the song is recognized for the singular contributions of George Harrison's sitar. Nevertheless, over time, the experimental nature of their music led to each of the Beatles pursuing more individualized tastes and preferences. The benefits of staying in the band dissipated. Indeed, the band became an artistically constraining organizational structure. These effects are different from the experience of the Rolling Stones and the Beach Boys, which has found the organizational structure to be critical to their continuation as an ongoing commercial enterprise. Moreover, while the Jagger/Richards combination continued to produce innovation on the artistic side, the effects on innovation of staying together diminished.

References

Gammell, Caroline. 2011. "Rolling Stones Envied The Beatles' Singing Prowess—Sir Paul." *The Telegraph*, May 23. Retrieved from www.telegraph.co.uk/culture/music/music-news/8531033/Rolling-Stones-envied-The-Beatles-singing-prowess-Sir-Paul.html, last accessed October 6, 2019.

Langley, William. 2013. "Mick Jagger: The Rolling Stone Who Changed Music." *The Telegraph*, July 26. Retrieved from www.telegraph.co.uk/culture/music/rolling-stones/10192279/Mick-Jagger-the-Rolling-Stone-who-changed-music.html, last accessed October 4, 2019.

Margotin, Philippe and Jean-Michel Guesdon. 2016. *The Rolling Stones: The Story Behind Every Track*. New York: Black Dog & Leventhal.

Martin, George. 2009. *All You Need Is Ears*. New York: St. Martin's Press.

Morgan, Johnny. 2015. *The Beach Boys: America's Band*. New York: Sterling.

Richards, Keith. 2010. *Life*. New York: Back Bay Books.

Rolling Stone. 2010. "100 Greatest Artists of All Time." Retrieved from www.rollingstone.com/music/music-lists/100-greatest-artists-147446/bob-dylan-10-31068, last accessed October 3, 2019.

The Rolling Stones. 2003. *According to the Rolling Stones*, ed. Dora Loewenstein, Philip Dodd, and Charlie Watts. New York: Chronicle Books.

Smucker, Tom. 2018. *Why the Beach Boys Matter*. Austin, TX: University of Texas Press.

Van Zandt, Steven. 2010. "100 Greatest Artists: No. 4: The Rolling Stones." Retrieved from www.rollingstone.com/music/music-lists/100-greatest-artists-147446/the-rolling-stones-6-30731, last accessed October 6, 2019.

Wilson, Brian. 2016. *I Am Brian Wilson: A Memoir*. New York: De Capo Press.

7

ECONOMIC REFLECTIONS FROM THE AFTERLIFE

So, were the Beatles the black swan of popular music? Undoubtedly, their music was path-breaking and influential. They were the touch point for the British Invasion that swept American culture in the 1960s and 1970s. But the economic lens used to analyze their rise and sustained success casts doubt on whether they were truly a Black Swan—an unlikely or improbable event difficult to predict but has a game changing impact. Indeed, one could argue (and some have) that the Beatles were just riding a wave of economic prosperity. If the Beatles didn't benefit, another band would have stepped into the void. The Rolling Stones, in fact, probably did more to change the economic model of the industry to reward artists than the Beatles. Certainly, their prodigious output and influence as a rock band suggests they had the stamina, drive, and ambition.

Moreover, the Beatles had few of the artistic core elements that would suggest their impact on music would be so transformative. None of the individual Beatles were gifted musicians to begin with. Their talent was cultivated through hard work, dedication to their craft, and grit. They lacked formal training. They did not grow up in households that could invest substantial resources into their musical hobbies. They were from northern England, almost completely disconnected from the entertainment industry leaders in London. They suffered personal loss or debilitating illnesses at early ages that might have crippled them emotionally and developmentally. Even some of their most creative and enduring works were inspired by the creative efforts of others in the industry. Other bands such as Rory Storm and the Hurricanes, the Vipers, and Gerry and the Pacemakers were also gaining momentum as the skiffle craze turned into British rock and roll.

The economic lens, however, suggests that the Beatles were not just in the right place at the right time. They were entrepreneurs with an intuitive sense of economics, strategic management, and resource use. Their decision making reflected a keen understanding of the need to ensure the right people are on the team to be productive. Playing together over extended periods allowed them to develop their skills. These skills allowed them to create a foundation of knowledge and competence that served as a springboard to creating value in other areas of pop music. In short, they engaged in "strategic entrepreneurship" to use these resources to identify new opportunities and create value. Thus, through the Hamburg residencies and subsequent concerts and tours of England, they developed a sound that was distinct from their contemporaries. Their energy and charisma on stage combined with tight performances, rock and roll sound that blended their instruments, and vocal harmonies set them apart from their competitors. As their long-time record producer George Martin observed: their value was in the band, not a particular individual who could front the group. This sound resonated forcefully with a largely ignored but burgeoning consumer market of youth, first in England, then America, and then the world. This expanding consumer market was a necessary but not sufficient condition for their success.

The Beatles added a second component that allowed them to strike a different trajectory from their competitors: An entrepreneurial, or growth, mindset. John Lennon set the tone early on, reinforced by Paul McCartney, that the band had to offer more than their competitors as well as something new compared to what they produced before. This mindset became particularly prevalent when they started to climb the charts in the UK and their popularity on concert tours expanded. While the Hamburg residencies were critical for improving their musicianship and performance skills, their decision to learn the B-sides of popular artists, add their own spin (or riff) to the songs they played, and eventually add their own songs to the line-up were geared to further their success as a group. This emphasis on "the new" created an internal culture of song craftsmanship and recording that was fundamentally focused on innovation.

In an interview with the English talk show host David Frost in 2012, Paul McCartney remembers this process was good for establishing the expectations of the group and easing the individual band members into their growing roles:

> The good thing about the Beatles' career is that it was a staircase. While now you'll get kids come in at the top—like *American Idol, We've Got Talent, X Factor*—and over a period of 8 weeks they are major national stars. Well, we couldn't get arrested at first. So we would play little clubs. And then we would play Hamburg, then we'd play ballrooms, then theaters, then the telly, then by the time the screaming came we were used to it.

Lennon and McCartney's role as creative gatekeepers was not purely, or even largely, self-centered. This was particularly evident as the band shifted to original song recording. They applied the same rules to their own songs as they did others in the group. In essence, a proposed song had to pass two thresholds to be considered. First, was the song offering something new and different? When they were writing original material, the question they asked was whether the same song, chord progression, or sound had already been done before. While the sound could be inspired by another artist (e.g., the Byrds, the Yardbirds, Chuck Berry, the Beach Boys, etc.), the song has to build to something different and new. Second, the song has to sound good. Aesthetics and the experience of the listener matter. While later contributions, such as the sound collage on *The Beatles* (the *White Album*) that forms the core of "Revolution 9," arguably stretched the boundaries on this second criterion, the rule was still applied. The track wasn't a random mix of sounds, but arranged to create a specific aesthetic, albeit an experimental one. (Notably, Paul McCartney was thinking about contributing a sound collage and was somewhat disappointed that John Lennon had beaten him to it.) While vinyl albums had limited space, the goal was to ensure the best songs made it onto the album. Lennon and McCartney were not immune to these rules.

This commitment to innovation continued well after the break-up of the band. McCartney worked diligently and steadily after 1970 to define a new sound that was distinct from the Beatles. He achieved this objective, he has said, when he completed *Band on the Run*. He also performed classical music, his first composition written on commission by the Liverpool Oratorio on commission from the Royal Liverpool Philharmonic Society in 1991. Lennon, for his part, continued to produce high quality music, releasing *John Lennon/Plastic Ono Band* (1970) and *Imagine* (1971) to critical acclaim. His album *Double Fantasy* was voted Album of the Year at the Grammy awards (after his death).

George Harrison's post-Beatles work was also substantial. *All Things Must Pass* is considered evidence of the bottled-up talent ready to be released upon the break-up. He continued to have significant success, producing the world's first global benefit rock concert with the Concert for Bangladesh, charting additional number one singles ("My Sweet Lord," "Give Me Love," "Got My Mind Set On You"), extensive collaborations with leading artists, and co-founding the "supergroup" the Traveling Wilburys (with Jeff Lynne, Bob Dylan, Roy Orbison, and Tom Petty).

Ringo Starr was always more performance-based, preferring a more clearly pop-defined musical style. Yet he also recorded (with the help of George Harrison) two number one songs on the Billboard charts: "You're Sixteen" and "Photograph." Eight songs made it into the top 10 of the Billboard Hot 100. Most importantly, each of the Beatles has been inducted into the Rock and Roll Hall of Fame as solo artists, recognizing their work independently of the Beatles.

Some have argued that Lennon, McCartney, Harrison, and Starr did their best work while in the Beatles. This is not necessarily the case, and the economic perspective shows why. The Beatles, as an organization and group, had become creatively stifling for the individual band members. In fact, all the band members continued to collaborate outside the formal structure of the band after the break-up. The exception was collaboration between John Lennon and Paul McCartney. But Lennon and McCartney were also exploring very different musical styles and aesthetics. All the Beatles successfully moved on from their band days artistically, adding significant creative content and pushing the boundaries of pop music in different ways. This is unlikely to have happened if the band had stayed together.

Paradoxically, an economic view suggests conventional wisdom about the impact and importance of the break up is turned on its head. Each of the individual Beatles benefited from being released from an increasingly dysfunctional and unproductive organizational structure. Their fans, and popular music, likely benefited significantly from the break-up because the Beatles were free to use their wealth and influence to break through the shibboleths of popular music that imposed too many constraints on individual artists.

Ironically, the economic approach to art and innovation that creates the bedrock of this book validates much of what the Beatles said at the time of their break-up. Paul McCartney, in an interview with evening talk show host Larry King, remembered, "We were still good musically. You know we were just maybe a little bit tense as friends now." For McCartney, the "essence" was "I think it was time." The rest of the world was growing up. "I always remember the old song 'wedding bells are breaking up that old gang of mine,' you know," he continued, drawing on the metaphors of everyday life that are so important to his songwriting. "The army buddies—the band. And you're going to grow up, you're going to get married, you're going to get girlfriends and have babies and things. You don't do that in a band." George Harrison echoed the same sentiment in an interview with talk show host Dick Cavett immediately following the break-up.

Economics works best when it helps explain the world of everyday life. Economics is the science of choice under constraints. In the case of the Beatles, the economic framework provides a useful lens for teasing out more of the nuances and layers behind the entrepreneurship of popular music. The Beatles had unprecedented influence on popular culture and art, and they deserve their legendary status. Economics, however, brings the myth in alignment with the realities of markets, consumer preferences, and the foundations of an entrepreneurial culture and its impacts.

SUBJECT INDEX

SONG AND ALBUM INDEX

Note: album titles are in italics.

Printed in the United States
by Baker & Taylor Publisher Services